From Baldwin King
Cheryl L. A. King

With best wishes
10/13/07

QUEST FOR CARIBBEAN UNITY:
BEYOND COLONIALISM

ESSAYS
TAKEN FROM FLAMBEAU MAGAZINE
(1965-68)


EDITED BY

KENNETH JOHN BALDWIN KING
CHERYL L. A. KING


KINGS-SVG

PUBLISHED BY

KINGS-SVG
BOX 702, MADISON, NJ 07940, USA
AND
BOX 2713, ST VINCENT AND THE GRENADINES
www.kingsinn-svg.com

QUEST FOR CARIBBEAN UNITY:
BEYOND COLONIALISM

COPYRIGHT 2006 BY KINGS-SVG

ISBN: 0-9778981-1-3

PUBLICATION DATE: NOVEMBER 2006

PRINTED IN THE USA BY

WIPF AND STOCK PUBLISHERS
199 WEST 8 TH AVENUE, SUITE 3
EUGENE, OREGON 97401

COVER PHOTO: FORT CHARLOTTE
ST. VINCENT AND THE GRENADINES
COURTESY: CHERYL L. A. KING

# CONTENTS

1. The Guyanese Situation by Kenneth John  1
2. The Federal Idea and West Indies Political Association by Kenneth John  7
3. Customs Union and the Little Seven by Wallace Dear  15
4. Footnotes on Slavery by Kenneth John  21
5. On Afro-West Indian Thinking by Kerwyn Morris  31
6. Issues in the Jamaica-Windwards Banana War by George Beckford  35
7. Gary Sobers and the Brisbane Revolution by Woodville Marshall  43
8. Independence, Unity and Non-Alignment by Kerwyn Morris  55
9. Historical Materialism and Caribbean Destiny by Kerwyn Morris  61
10. Social and Economic Problems in the Windward Islands by Woodville Marshall  69
11. Education and Social Goals by Kenneth John  77
12. Some Political Aspects of Independence by E. Augustus and W. Rodney  83
13. Economic Integration in Central America by John W. Crow  89
14. The Future Role of Caribbean Youth by Kenneth John  99
15. The Day I Saw Forbes Burnham by F. W. Dowers  107
16. The Children of Sisyphus - A Review by Karl John  109
17. Some Aspects of Scientific Philosophy by Baldwin King  113
18. The Democratic Process and the Single Party in the New States by Daniel Williams  121
19. He Defended Euro-American Imperialism and Exploitation by Kerwyn Morris  129
20. Man and His Religion by Marcia Harold  133
21. Obstacles to Economic Growth by Arnhim Eustace  139
22. Ideological Sanity by Cedric Harold  147
23. The School and the Community by Claudon Fraser  153
24. Reflections on Race Relations in the USA by Jean Norris  159
25. C. L. R. James-The Man and His Work by Martin Glaberman  167

26. On Facing Realities in Economics and Politics by Cedric Harold 171
27. A Teacher's Life and Terms by Marcia Harold   177
28. Beyond a Boundary – A Review by Timothy Hector   181
29. Slavery – Total Institution or Total System by Castine Quashie 185
30. Some Facts About Yugoslavia by Oskar Novak   193

## CONTRIBUTORS

Earl Augustus
George Beckford
John W. Crow
F. W. Dowers
Arnhim Eustace
Claudon Fraser
Martin Glaberman
Cedric Harold
Marcia Harold
Timothy Hector
Karl John
Kenneth John
Baldwin King
Woodville Marshall
Kerwyn Morris
Jean Norris
Oskar Novak
Castine Quashie
Walter Rodney
Daniel Williams

# ACKNOWLEDGEMENTS

We would like to thank all the authors of these essays or their representatives for their permission to republish these articles. We also thank Ms Carol Alfone of New Jersey for painstakingly typing the manuscript. Thanks also to Debra King and Dr. Cherene King for their help in formatting and putting the finishing touches on the manuscript.

This volume is dedicated to the memory of the members and associates of the original Kingstown Study Group, St. Vincent and the Grenadines, who have passed away – Daniel Williams, Claudon Fraser, Eddie Griffith, Timothy Daisy, John Velox, Alphonso Roberts, Joyce Peters, Edgerton Richards and Henry Williams.

x

## PREFACE

In 1964, a group of young Vincentian intellectuals formed themselves into the Kingstown Study Group. Among the aims of the organization was to publish a quarterly magazine which was named "Flambeau" after the " torch that lit our ancestral way in those benighted days of slavery". The essays that dealt exclusively with St. Vincent and the Grenadines have been published under the title: "Search for Identity: Essays on St. Vincent and the Grenadines". This volume contains articles from Flambeau Magazine (1965-68) which have a distinctly Caribbean flavor and which comprise the first half of the book. The second half contains the remainder of the articles of a philosophical, religious or sociological nature.

In the early 1960's, we had just experienced the break-up of the West Indies Federation. Jamaica, Trinidad and Barbados became politically independent but many of the smaller islands remained under the yoke of colonialism. In spite of the factionalism, many of us in the Group still felt the need for the islands to unite in some fashion for mere survival. Some of the essays reflected that sentiment and so we have titled this volume: "Quest For Caribbean Unity: Beyond Colonialism" in the firm belief that the islands of the Caribbean, particularly the English-Speaking countries, must unite for their own salvation in this era of globalization. CARICOM (Caribbean Community) and the OECS (Organization of Eastern Caribbean States) are positive moves in this direction and the recent introduction of the CSME (Caribbean Single Market and Economy) is especially encouraging. However there is still much to be done before we can consider ourselves fully integrated, with no less than a political union as the ultimate realization of our indivisible unity. We hope that this and succeeding generations of Caribbean people will rise to the occasion.

Baldwin King  
Kenneth John  
Cheryl L. A. King

November, 2006

# The Guyanese Situation

## By KENNETH JOHN

(Taken from Flambeau, Number 1, June 1965)

(Note: Guyana used to be called British Guiana)

[Editor's Note: The following is the gist of a paper read at a group meeting and which formed the text of a radio talk given by Kenneth John after the Guianese general election of December 1964. In this article, Kenneth presents a succinct analysis of the background forces which he believes are forging the destiny of the trouble spot. He believes that the new electoral system of Proportional Representation which was introduced specifically to "destool" Jagan will eventually backfire. And he implies that a Guianese solution can only be brought about by a rapprochement between Jagan and Burnham, the leaders of the two major races.]

British Guiana (BG) has been much in the news for the past decade. As things stand, British Guiana might easily continue to occupy newspaper headlines for another ten years. For the dust from the last election in British Guiana has not nearly settled, as some unsophisticated people have gotten themselves to believe. Though it would be sheer folly to attempt prediction or prophecy in a highly fluid situation subject to constant change and the interplay of a miscellany of variables, it is only the naïve mind guilty of wishful thinking that will see the unholy alliance between the People's National Congress (PNC) and the United Front (UF), as offering the crowning answer and final solution to what has come to be known as the "The Guianese Problem." The fissure in Guianese society has gone, or rather has been dug too deep to be easily plastered over by constitutional impositions or a change in the voting system. It is as if some people think that you can recreate a society overnight, just as you had destroyed it when it suited you.

For it is going to be suggested here that the disquiet in British Guiana today and in the recent past has been primarily effected by outside forces with political axes to grind. The division of our shrinking political world into two hostile power blocs, call it the internationalization of politics if you want, has played havoc with colonial territories. Nowadays alien labels are stuck on colonial politicians before you can say "Jack Rabbit," and internal events are invariably stamped with external, usually irrelevant definitions. And so it has been with British Guiana where the social milieu offered immense scope for outside machinations, and rendered the country a mere pawn in the international chess game and its major races mere football between the ideologues of the two competing political camps.

The framework for the existing racial tension in British Guiana was set in the plantation society of the latter half of the 19$^{th}$ and early 20$^{th}$ century when Indian indentured servants replaced the emancipated negro as field workers on estates. The negro flocked into urban centers and the Indian occupied rural territory, thus underlying racial differences by an urban-rural cleavage. Reinforcing these divisive elements could be listed the following: The Indian was called in to do work the negro was glad to escape, resulting in negro contempt for "Coolie Labor". The ethnic differentiation of the Indian was perpetuated by the practice of endogamy (i.e, strict marriage within one's race) his cultural distinctiveness was underwritten by his acceptance of non-Christian faiths, and his "clannishness," which sprang from his closely knit kinship system, cut off the Indian from the total creole society to which the acculturated negro, driven from his African past, had unashamedly capitulated. So that whereas the Indian measured everything in Indian terms, the negro's standard of value was white with a capital "W" and thought by him superior. But though the Indian subsystem was marginal to the Guianese universe there was, at an early stage, a surprising amount of cooperation between negro and Indian, politically in parties and economically in trade unions. Not so surprisingly after all, if we reflect on the squalid conditions in which both races dwelt and the fact that they were welded together by the common goal of independence. It was only in the terminal stage of Colonialism when each group wished to guarantee its place in the sun and reserve some vantage point in the imminent new order that the cult of bi-racialism was born. Then the Indians became more assertive and, to the chagrin of the negro section, became education conscious, began to infiltrate the Civil Service and Teaching profession hitherto jealously regarded as Negro monopolies. The negro became apprehensive of the spiraling Indian birth rate and the Indian feared a loss of identity in a largely Negro West Indian Federation. But before we analyze the present scene, let us attempt to put it in proper historical perspective.

We need not go further back than the mid 1940's to locate the historical beginnings of the social malaise which now strickens British Guiana. At this time, Guianese politicians were readying themselves for the resumption of the electoral process which was suspended over the war years. In 1946, Dr. Singh's Labor Party attempted to represent an amalgam of the various racial groups in British Guiana, but the party lost the 1947 elections hands down, Dr. Cheddi Jagan being the only winner in a predominantly Negro district. The Labor Party disintegrated and Cheddi Jagan formed the P.A.C., a small agitational group which defined Guianese problems within a Marxist term of reference. The post-war period was characterized by industrial strife symbolized in the Enmore riots of 1948 when five striking sugar workers were shot to death by the Police. This incident, a common event in most colonial territories, was compounded by the accidental element of race – that the workers were Indians and the policemen negro. We can probably take time off to record some of the repercussions which this unfortunate state of the country's occupational structure has caused.

The occupational structure so far from easing race tension (as it has done in Trinidad where both races were more or less knit together in one embracing industrial complex) has tended to harden racial attitudes into assuming uncompromising, intransigent positions, so that a largely negro middle class, including the civil service, can strike against the Kaldor Budget on the grounds that "forced savings" were not going to affect the peasantry who happen to be Indians. When Dr. Jagan attempts to diversify the economy he is accused of championing the cause of rice farmers who, incidentally were Indians; a predominantly negro police force can be charged with taking sides during race riots, and so on and so forth. This built-in tendency to race suspicion inherent in Guianese society has been used by external forces who have a vested interest in a chronic state of political instability in British Guiana which would warrant the indefinite postponement of independence.

To return to the more strictly political development, the P.A.C. mentioned above proved to be the precursor of the larger and more impressive P.P.P. to which it was inflated in 1950. Among the members were the Jagans, Forbes Burnham and Sydney King. The P.P.P. was originally a broad coalition of racial groups operating on a socialist platform, and Dr. Jagan could announce that the enemies of the party included East Indians Associations, and the league of colored people, and he could denounce the opposing N.D.P. as a coalition of Negro racialists and Portuguese business interests. One would have thought that the P.P.P., a party transcending race, was a God-send for British Guiana and that its sweeping victory in 1953 was a good augury for the future of the country, but this was not to be so.

After what Ashton Chase has chosen to call "133 days towards Freedom," the Government was discredited, the Constitution suspended, and Governor's rule substituted. Two years later the P.P.P. was split right down the middle into Jaganite and Burnhamite factions, called P.P.P.-J. and P.P.P.-B. The Jaganites won the 1959 election under the makeshift Renison Constitution and in 1959 Burnham renamed his party Peoples Natonal Congress. The P.P.P. again won the 1961 election. Anti-Jagan forces observed that, over the years the P.P.P. won a disproportionate number of seats in relation to individual votes cast for it and the British Government acceded to the request that the electoral system be altered to the Proportional Representation method, reputed as a vicious and iniquitous sytsem for dividing peoples, producing weak coalition Governments and ensuring unstable politics.

In 1953, we recall, the broadly based P.P.P. which embraced both major ethnic groups had carried all before it at the polls. Such a powerful, well organized grouping was anathema to certain so-called free countries, this side of the Iron Curtain. If one were to start with the premise that Jagan is believed to be Communist and must be got rid of at all costs, then subsequent events read like a logical sequel. On the announcement of the P.P.P. victory, Columnist Drew Pearson commented in the "Daily Mirror," "The wires were busy between Washington and Whitehall as to what should be done to stop the establishment of a Communist bridge-head in South America which would pose a threat to the Panama Canal." It was in this atmosphere of Red hysteria generated from the U.S. and forming a colonial extension of the McCarthy witch hunts which then bedeviled the American political scene that one must understand the suspension of the Guianese Constitution, which in turn triggered off the race conflict that has snowballed into the monstrous proportions we witness today. The charges against the Government could hardly past muster among political analysts so much so that Harold McMillan had to resort to speaking only about their cumulative effect, and James Griffith could remark, "Some things have been brought into the White Paper which, quite frankly, I think gives the impression of scraping the barrel for evidence." The most revealing expose came, however, from the circumstances in British Guiana itself. On the day in which troops descended to uncover an arson plot and prevent a Communist takeover, an inter-colonial cricket match between British Guiana and Trinidad took place without incident.

The Robertson Commission justified the suspension, but that was the least thing it did. By dichotomising the P.P.P. members into Communists and Socialists, the Commission drove a wedge into the Nationalist Movement that was the P.P.P. The Jagans were branded Communists and Burnham was declared to be mildly Socialist. At the same time, it stated further that British Guiana could not hope for political advancement under the present leadership. Taking the cue, Burnham split the Party in the following year. Small wonder that Jaganites have believed that the Commission utilized the very effective weapon of divide and rule in its report. For, --and this is significant--, the fissure originally represented a power struggle with a very subsidiary ideological component consisting of methods of approach with a basic agreement on fundamentals. In fact to this very day, Burnham for all practical purposes stands on all ideological fours with Jagan. The initial schism was also inter-racial in character but once the split occurred, the logic of the situation drove the protagonists apart on the racial issues and led to the emergence of the racial factor as the prominent feature on the political landscape.

In the 1957 elections when the Jaganites were reported to have used the slogan, "Apan Jaat," i.e., vote race, in its house to house campaigning, through to the 1961 elections when Sydney King called for the division of British Guiana into a Negro and Indian Section after the fashion of India and Pakistan, the race element became obtrusive. So much so that the voting trend has more or less ossified into a stereotyped pattern. Jagan depend on the Indians in the Sugar Belt, rice farmers along the coast and the Indian business interest whom he accommodated. The bulk of the P.N.C.'s support comes from African Workers in Georgetown, New Amsterdam and the principal mining town of McKenzie, together with secondary support from the police force and civil servants U.F. voters are comprised mainly of Portuguese businessmen, other minority groups and the Roman Catholic Amerindians.

With the P.P.P. victory in 1961 and the real prospect of independence looming around the corner, matters were brought to the head. The Kaldor Budget which was commended by development economists the world over and praised by highly reputed Western newspapers as the N.Y. Times and the London Times, was used as a peg on which to hang a number of irrelevant issues and sparked off the magazine of race riots and a crippling civil servants strike. Similarly the Labor relations Bill which has been patterned off the U.S. Wagner Act was the excuse for more strikes and riots. Independence conferences invariably ended in deadlock. Jagan could neither extract aid from the

Western Countries nor obtain British permission to accept Eastern assistance to bolster his crumbling strife torn economy. Asked about prospects for Independence in the U.N. in 1963, Jagan referred his interviewers to President Kennedy, at once indicating the deep involvement of the U.S. in British Guiana's affairs. Then the British, past masters in colonial strategy, pounced upon the idea of Proportional Representation which they apparently anticipated would produce a proliferation of parties, break Jagan's strength and necessitate coalition. The result of the recent election, therefore, was a calculated gain. Whatever one may say, it remains crystal clear that it is impossible for men of the likes of Burnham and D'Aiguar to be harnessed between the same political shafts for any decent length of time. British Guiana might enjoy the brief respite from internal strife while storm clouds gather on both sides for a final outburst. For no "settlement," so called, which ignores either of the country's two major races can pretend to inspire confidence or produce peace. There can be no progress within a divided country and the present Guianese situation indicates that the two races might have been freed, but a society has not been allowed to evolve.

**Dr Kenneth John holds a Ph.D. in Political Science from Manchester University. He is a newspaper columnist and a practicing lawyer in St Vincent and the Grenadines.**

## 2 THE FEDERAL IDEA AND WEST INDIAN POLITICAL ASSOCIATION

By Kenneth John

(Taken from Flambeau, Number 2, September 1965)

    The political atmosphere seems to be suffused with talk of West Indian Federation, Little Eight or "Lucky Seven," Unitary Statehood with Trinidad, Unitary State of the Windward Islands, association with Canada or U.S., going it alone, secession and what have you – enough to challenge the usefulness of afflicting our innocent people with more sterile talk on a seemingly overused theme and belabored subject. But the simple reason at the back of this paper is this: that the various forms of political association are not academic issues which float about in high intellectual altitudes and are the monopoly of an esoteric club of that peculiar brood of men called politicians; political contrivances derive their rationale from the part they play in making human life more worthwhile and are geared to the pursuit of the Good Life, and political issues must therefore be put squarely before the people's tribunal for their verdict, moreso when our political future seems so misty. We are assuming that, despite all the empty sermonization on the various forms of political combinations, the people have been precluded from discussion of the concepts, that in all the arrangements made for the establishment of changing political structures, the people have remained passive spectators, that decisions fashioning the destiny of the area have been conceived, processed, and resolved around conference tables without reference to the people. And it is our conviction that, without active popular participation, without mass involvement at every level of political discussion, the resultant structure would be unreal and artificial, lacking that vitality which springs only from the emotional investment of the people who are the flesh and blood of all political contrivance.

    The West Indian historical scene has long been punctuated with notions about federation, confederation and association. Recently there has been a federal experiment which never came off the ground floor, and today there have been half-hearted attempts to fashion another federation which seems to have died stillborn, and with it the very real danger that the idea of federation might atrophy. And this trend is not surprising when we reflect on the little contact, the lamentable absence of any meaningful dialogue, between the architects of the federal structure and its owners; in other words, the sad lack of communion between the elected and their electors. Way back in 1878, an old woman in Barbados who had missed seeing the Prince of Wales during a visit remarked – so Eric Williams tells it – that she would make sure and get a glimpse of Federation whenever he arrived. This abysmal ignorance about political forms still obtains among West Indians to this very day. In the Jamaican Referendum campaign on the Federal issue in 1961, the leading anti-federationist could sway the emotions of a credulous audience with the preposterous remark that the federal ships were sent to take them back to slavery and that federation meant literal enslavement. Similarly the bulk of our people do not have the foggiest idea as to the meaning of the federal idea, what are its advantages, when it is appropriate. Most other federations were preceded by the political education of the masses on the federal principle in which the various ideas were thoroughly canvassed, the concept discussed, and the relative advantages of the nuances of its competing forms argued. Not so in the West Indies. From the word go, the idea has been elitist in origin and execution, with all decisions emanating from the top in one-way traffic. On the eve of what was piously hoped might be the formal launching of the Federal Ship of State – "H.M.S. LITTLE EIGHT"-- a colonial secretary could refer to the whole exercise as "shrouded in a veil of secrecy," in which, of course, it was. So our first major point is that, as beneficiaries of a political trust, the people must be well versed on all the things that are done in their name, must be briefed on what is happening – as it happens – and must, first of all, be made to know what federation is, and why it has been chosen as their political destiny.

For the moment, since it affords us a reasonable point of departure, we will follow the line of least resistance and accept (though with reservations) the classical definition of the term according to the gospel of Professor K.C. Wheare, whose "Federal Government" is widely accepted as the bible of federalism. Wheare claims that a federation is an "association of states so organized that powers are divided between a general government which in certain matters is independent of the governments of the associated states, and, on the other hand, state governments which, in certain matters, are, in turn, independent of the general government." Alternatively, we may say that federations set up two tiers of government, at the regional and local level, both of which are committed, so to speak, to walking a political tight rope which is assiduously watched and refereed by an impartial judiciary. The division of government is a matter of strict bargaining, though the area of common interest generally falls within the powers of the federal Government – the so-called Exclusive list – while the rest of the items lapse to the unit territories and constitute the Residual List. Nowadays it is fashionable to have a third list, the Concurrent List, on which both Governments can legislate with this proviso, that in the event of conflict, the local legislature must give way to the Federal Government.

Another way of looking at "Federation" is to compare it with the Unitary system of Government in which a central legislature lords it over the local government bodies such as village and town councils and municipal boards. If St. Vincent were a federation, then the local bodies would exist as of their own right and not live by the grace of the central authority. But if, as Wheare would have it, independent existence is the touchstone of federalism, then we are likely to encounter a wide margin of definitional imprecision, a sort of twilight zone of doubt as to which system of Government certain states operate. Wheare uncharitably consigns a large group of states to a category called quasi-federal.

Nothing is wrong with the approach if we bear in mind that, because something does not fit neatly into a conceptual model, does not make it "abnormal" or "fraudulent", since states devise systems of government which can best answer their problems and not political forms which can be nicely labeled. So that, for instance, South Africa attempts to meet its needs by a decentralized unitary government while India does more or less the same thing in her tightly-knit federation and it is academic whether one is a federation and the other is not. And this argument is not spuriously disputatious or guilty of linguistic quibbling but has serious implications for constitution makers. Time and again, the debates on the structure of the First West Indies Federation were really textbook pontification, that if such and such a measure were passed, then we could not call our federation a federation and so forth. So what? As if government is a function of constitutions and not of societies, as if politics is determined by the paper document which constitutional lawyers draw up to map its course and not by the social make-up of the particular country. Yet this amateurish approach and slavish attachment to bookish concepts and sterile categories still persist. Barbados in issuing a White Paper to justify her policy of going it alone cites the St. Lucia stand which demands more central control of the purse strings as doing "considerable violence to the federal principle of coordinate and independent authority." And the paper lays the further claim that reads like a charge that "the position taken by the Government of St. Lucia is more consistent with a condition of unitary statehood than with a Federal system of association," which is precisely the point to which any meaningful twentieth century federation must approximate!

In fact the Wheare definition of Federation which sets a premium on the independence of the unit territories is inapplicable to a developing nation today. The Wheare concept is historically provincial and culture bound; it is dated and geographically restricted. It belongs to the 18$^{th}$ and 19$^{th}$ century Western Countries of poor communication and isolated communities which were propelled by political philosophies calling for weak governments, entrenchment of "State Rights" and a dispersal of power. Government was accordingly split into water-tight compartments, into insulated chambers. In this modern age the changing times have set in motion certain centripetal forces to operate in the old federations by which more and more power has been progressively gravitating to the center at the expense of the circumference. War, economic depression and notions of the welfare state have had a centralizing effect on the classical federations so that North Ireland, in the unitary state of the U.K., for example, enjoys as much local autonomy as any of the Australian States, which must make nonsense of the Wheare dichotomy. The new federations have generally approximated close to the classical unitary state. The quest for total solidarity in countries afflicted with cultural diversities and divided loyalties, the prevalence of one party systems and the dominance of charismatic leadership, the appeal of socialism and constant fear of hydra-headed colonialism, and the unitary psychology which springs from the fact that some are really federations in reverse (India and Nigeria), have all rendered the modern day federation so tight as to blur the line of demarcation from the unitary state.

The question now revolves around the idea of a West Indian federation. It seems as though the First Federation was in part killed by the crossfire of the classical and modern schools of thought as represented by Jamaica and Trinidad respectively, and the "Little Eight," now awaiting its coup de grace, has been strangled by the opposing views of Antigua and St. Lucia. Wherever there is a tradition of insularity, and the West Indies abounds with this, there is a need of a strong and powerful center to streamline differences and blunt the edges of parochialism, to act as a countervailing power to what Gordon Lewis has termed "the fissiparous tendency of the localist mentality." Otherwise the federation will tear apart at its seams, as indeed our First Federation disintegrated, because of duplication, entrenchment of local prejudices, administrative bungling, and dog-in-the-manger fights without the remedial features of rational economic planning and a real coordination. In arguing the case for a strong center in the First Federation, the Prime Minister's Office of Trinidad put it this way in the "Economics of Nationhood": 'These islands have a long history of insularity rooted in the historical development of their economy and trade, and the difficulties of communication for centuries. No amount of subjective, that is to say, historical, cultural or other activity of the times can be expected to overcome this heritage. Only a powerful and centrally directed economic coordination and interdependence can create the true foundations of a nation. Barbados will not unify with St. Kitts, or Trinidad with British Guiana, or Jamaica with Antigua. They will be knit together only through their common allegiance to a central government. Anything else will discredit the conception of Federation and leave the islands more divided than before." Prophetic words with their author being among the instruments of their realization! Indeed it has been reasonably argued that the West Indies is a natural unitary area and that a strong federation is only a second best. The advocates of loose federation often argue about our cosmopolitanism when we are eighty percent Afro-Asian, they speak about our differences, of our various identities when we are fairly homogenous in terms of religion and language, they talk glibly of economic disparities where we are all poor, and of our separation by sea when a Sun-Jet can run through the entire West Indian archipelago in between two successive meals. One has only to look at Ghana, Kenya, Burma and Indonesia where solid nations have been formed under a single government even while separatist opposition forces – with more justification than in the West Indian case – have clamored unsuccessfully for federalism in which they hoped to preserve their little pockets of provincial and tribal resistance to national mobilization. Or take a massive and culturally diverse region like Nigeria, linguistically – torn Pakistan, whose wings are separated by a thousand miles or Indian territory, or India which is a world unto itself, regions which, admittedly with some strain, do operate a strong federation and immediately the pettifogging and bickering over the pros and cons of a West Indian federation dissolve into mere empty chatter.

But politics being the art of the possible, unitary state of a wider West Indian nation or of the Little Eight is virtually taboo. In fact, politicians fear that a strong federal center will prove a sort of Frankenstein monster. The truth is that our leaders are mortally afraid of the whittling away of their local seats of power which a unitary state or strong federation, albeit the sole salvation for these colonies, entail. No one cherishes the idea of declaring his post redundant or planning his own obsolescence (least of all politicians) and the establishment of either of these forms of association involves the demise of a substantial slice of our present leadership. As far back as 1936, Arthur Lewis, in a paper to the British Fabian Society, affirmed that "the real stumbling block has been the opposition of local potentates, fearful that their voices, all powerful in a small island, will be unheard in a large federation." This statement, more than any other, gives the reasons behind the present stalemate surrounding West Indian association and gives the lie to the fatuous official statements about providing for "our children and our children's children," and so forth, while myopic Ministers of Government continue to feather their own nest and jealously safeguard their sinecures.

The old federation is as dead as a "dodo". The Little Eight – or Lucky Seven, have your pick – is on its deathbed. But mere survival demands that the islands of the West Indies unite in some form or shape. England wants to be rid of us for we are a constant embarrassment in this world of decolonization and, what's more, the West Indian sponge has been squeezed dry. Continued colonial status is also anathema to all progressive thinking West Indians who, in the tradition of Africa, prefer mismanaged self-rule to proper colonial office control. A link-up with a negro-hating country like America is unthinkable as we cannot afflict that "Leader of the Free Nations" with the million headaches which one of her presidents once called us. Association with Canada is unpalatable if we aspire to being something more than a nation of domestic servants. If chronically bad West Indian Leadership persists, then a last recourse might be had in the assumption of some measure of autonomy under the wings of the U.N. But first, a determined effort must be made to salvage the West Indies by working out some sort of political formula for association. We may not be able to define or quantify our political aspirations, but we feel and recognize them all the same. We share a common heritage, suffer a common fund of hardships and have broadly similar aims; and we know that in this world of political combines, ideological blocs and economic unions that if we do not hang together, we will hang separately. Elsewhere someone has told us of the benefits which are likely to accrue from association for economic ends. The submission here is that political association will enhance these: more aid-giving countries are likely to come forward and deal with one solidly effective government of the region than deal separately with a plethora of self-opinionated miniscule legislatures; the proposed West Indian economic community needs a political executive authority to enforce decisions, coordinate, and dilute by planning, the lopsided development consequent upon the impersonal response to naked economic dictation; and one integrated West Indian bloc will be taken more seriously in the councils of the world. Nkrumah's dictum of "seeking first the political kingdom...." still stands. It seems as though a federation of British Guiana, Trinidad, Barbados, a Unitary Windward Islands and a Unitary Leeward Islands is the best thing that can happen to the West Indies today. But it is going to be rough business. As was intimated earlier, the West Indian politician who must take the initiative, has a vested interest in the status quo – a gullible people, a fat salary, a position of influence in a fairly advanced constitution, and ultimate colonial office financial responsibility. Thus caught in a vicious circle, our political future remains one huge, frightening, question mark. Among the first of the British Colonies, we have succeeded in remaining the last. The umbilical chord which ties us to the British connection, just would not give; nothing colonizes like colonialism. But something will give – some day.

**Dr Kenneth John holds a Ph.D. in Political Science from Manchester University. He is a newspaper columnist and a practicing lawyer in St Vincent and the Grenadines**

Quest for Caribbean Unity

## 3   CUSTOMS UNION AND THE LITTLE SEVEN

By Wallace Dear

(Taken from Flambeau, Number 2, September 1965)

Interest in the topic -- Customs Union -- is no doubt aroused by the fact that the Regional Council of Ministers has requested a rather early examination of and report on the problem. The early attention it has received leads us to think that not only is the matter being seriously considered, but also that its introduction may be either simultaneous with, or following shortly upon, the proposed Federation of the Seven. It may be recorded here that even at the dissolution of the last West Indies Federation, Customs Union had not been introduced. Unfortunately, there has been no public discussion of Customs Union and consequently, many persons are ignorant of what it means or why it should be considered. This is perhaps partly explained by the dearth of professional economists in the area, and the absence of "economic journalism" which attempts to shed light on current economic matters.

This short paper attempts to do three things: firstly to define clearly what is meant by Customs Union; secondly to present the arguments in favor of a Customs Union; and lastly to consider some of the problems concomitant with the introduction of Customs Union.

The term Customs Union is one which has been applied rather loosely to two closely related types of economic integration. According to paragraph (4) of Article 44 of the Havana Charter for an International Trade Organization:

"A Customs Union shall be understood to mean the substitution of a single customs territory for two or more Customs territories, so that –

(a) duties and other restrictive regulations of commerce.....are eliminated with respect to substantially all the trade between the constituent territories of the Union or at least with respect to substantially all the trade in products originating in such territories and

(b) substantially the same duties and other regulations of commerce are applied by each of the members of the Union to the trade of territories not included in the Union."

Customs Union is characterized by the substitution of a common external tariff for the various tariffs of each of the Units of the Federation. We may call it a Federal tariff which is common to goods and commodities imported from countries outside the Units. Another characteristic is the removal of tariff on the movement of goods between Units of the Federation which means, inter alia, that duty could only be levied once on goods entering from non-member countries. In addition we may note that no member of the Federation can impose a ban on goods from non-member countries except with the cooperation of the other units of the Federation. Indeed the formation of a federal state means that the capacity to affect international relationships has now been removed from the unit territories to the Federal Government. The above-mentioned union has been accurately referred to as a Federal Customs area.

This type of economic integration must be distinguished from another (also termed a Customs Union) of which the prototype is the European Economic Community. Here several units, agreeing to harmonize their customs tariffs and regulations in order to introduce free trade among themselves, merge their customs areas but retain separate political status and international identity. A study of this type of economic union reveals that it is somewhat inaccurate to speak of a common external tariff since there are as many tariffs as there are units participating, each tariff being a separate act of legislation by the member territory. Thus there is, in the European Common Market, a French tariff, and an Italian tariff, etc.

Such an arrangement should only be entered into if benefits are likely to be derived by any Unit. It is safe to assume that the government of the Units concerned have chosen, as a top priority, economic development of the islands. In this section we attempt to show that in our present condition we suffer many disadvantages which impede economic growth, and that Customs Union is one of the means of accelerating growth.

A striking feature, perhaps the most striking feature, of the Units of the proposed Federation which carries great economic significance, is their smallness. As a criterion of smallness, some economists have used the geographical size of the area; others, the size of the native population; still others have used the degree of dependence upon foreign markets with respect to both imports and exports – the greater the degree of dependence, the smaller the territory. The straight fact is that, whichever we choose to use, we cannot escape our smallness. Our smallness, in turn, contributes to three important disadvantages.

Firstly, it limits our economic power and the influence we can expect to exert on the international market. Our production of most commodities is such an infinitesimal part of world production that we cannot influence the market individually. The same is true of the goods that we import. However, with a united front, the chances of being able to attract attention on the market are greatly improved. Surely, if one instance may be quoted, the Windward Islands Banana Growers Association receives and will receive more attention than the same body in each of the Units concerned.

Secondly, our domestic market is not large enough to permit sale of the bulk of our production at home, and so protect ourselves to a large extent from economic fluctuations abroad. We therefore rely on foreign markets for disposal of our major crops to the extent that a change in demand, or world conditions, is certain to leave its mark on our economy.

Thirdly, we cannot take full advantage of the economies of large scale production. Again the size of the domestic market prevents the productive plants in many of our small industries from being used at near full capacity. Often such productive plants operate below the economic and technological optimum. This is a strong factor which discourages investors from investing their capital in many of the small islands particularly.

The advantages of Customs Union follow upon the introduction of Free Trade, which it is hoped will not only increase inter-territorial trade but also encourage new and greater investment in the area. Firstly, the removal of tariffs on locally produced goods means that they will now enjoy an advantage over imported goods of the same type. All things being equal, this should be an incentive to greater production since not only will there be a swing towards locally produced goods, but also a chance that some substitution will take place. Secondly the domestic market is increased to include the whole free trade area. Not only is the market larger, but it will be virtually assured, once every effort is made to increase inter-territorial trade.

The fact that the domestic market is both larger and assured should serve to encourage greater specialization. The advantages of specialization are obvious and need not be stressed. Suffice it to say that economies of scale should attract the type of investor who hitherto was reluctant to enter because no single island would have had a market large enough to make his venture profitable. In addition, larger concerns may find it advantageous to set up branches to enjoy the larger market. The above adds up to greater and varied economic activity within the area which is in itself an urgent necessity to relieve present economic strain, e.g., in unemployment to name only one.

There are many problems surrounding the introduction of Customs Union, but space only allows our dealing with a few. Most or perhaps all of the units are exporters of agricultural products, even though there are slight variations. All things being equal, the introduction of Customs Union is more problematic if the economies of the units concerned are competitive rather than complementary. The decision as to which country should produce a particular crop may not be reached very easily. However, on the other hand, the fact that many of these Units experience similar problems may well mean that efforts will be made to solve them on a regional rather than on a Unit level.

It has been voiced throughout the area that the only Unit likely to derive any benefits from the introduction of Customs Union is Barbados. The general consensus is that most of the industries will be attracted to Barbados, and for this reason there may be a reluctance in accepting Customs Union. One should here distinguish between short-run and long-run effects. There is little doubt that at the moment the industrial climate is likely to attract most of the investors into Barbados because it is more favorable than that of any of the other Units. However, in the long-run the concentration of industries in Barbados may place the other Units in a more attractive position relative to Barbados, with the result that an investment may now flow towards the other Units.

One of the major sources of Government revenue is import duties. There is every reason to believe that if the level of imports and tariff rates remain unchanged, the revenue from import duties will be lower with the introduction of Customs Union. While all import duties will be collected by the Federal Government, a certain percentage will be returned to the Unit Government. The problem I wish to draw attention to right here is that most of the expensive items will remain on the local budget while the most important source of Government revenue is being tapped. It may be that the very introduction of Customs Union will change both the level and pattern of imports.

Customs Union is a concomitant of Federation. While it is true that when the first Federation broke up, Customs Union had not yet been implemented, it is perhaps also true that this was the only example of Federation without Customs Union. It is unlikely that the proposed Federation of the Seven will be inaugurated without Customs Union for, inter alia, this is one of the ways of accelerating economic growth and emphasis seems to, or must, be placed on economic growth. However, a decision must be recorded one way or the other. Those who oppose Customs Union must face the task of suggesting an alternative. Shall we seek Union with the Unitary State of Trinidad and Tobago? Shall we seek some form of association with the U.S.A. or Canada? Shall we remain as colonies of Great Britain? Or shall we, with a strong will, urge ourselves to go it alone? Which shall it be?

**Wallace Dear is a retired economist and accountant and lives in Toronto, Canada.**

Quest for Caribbean Unity

# 4 FOOTNOTES ON SLAVERY

By Kenneth John

(Taken from Flambeau, Number 3, January 1966)

One can hardly think of a more emotive subject than slavery. Most of us, ashamed of our slave past, are prone to fight shy of any rational discussion on the topic, let bygones be bygones, we cry; others, preoccupied with sloganizing and finding comfort in easy stereotyped thinking see our every fault as some direct descendant of that bestial social institution called slavery; others with a careless manipulation of ideological symbols define our slave past simply as white-capitalist-imperialist domination of Black colonialist forces. We believe that no school of thought has a monopoly on truth about slavery and, in attempting a cool and objective analysis of the system as it affects us, we have interwoven selected strands of thought from the two latter schools. We wish to meet a need, the need to know the past in order to understand the present and plan for the future. In setting the records straight on our historical balance sheet, we try to avoid mis-emphases, insofar as it is humanly possible to do so, for whereas we hope that we are free of built-in biases, we do not pretend to make any vaunted claims to detachment; our involvement in the subject is too complete for that.

Many of our present day problems undoubtedly spring from a slave background. The first is psychological, the more dangerous and destructive since it is embedded within the bedrock of our own personality and operates on the subconscious plane. Slavery has left us with a crippling inferiority complex. We are ashamed of our past, of our race, and of our ancestral home, because we are taught that only an "inferior" people would subserve the interests of "superior" folk, that color and intelligence tend to vary inversely, i.e., the more colored the less intelligence, and that Africa whence most of us sprang was the Dark Continent from which we were rescued by philanthropic slave traders. Most of the beliefs which have been drummed into our heads during that long dark night and the longer more agonizing dusk in which we still exist are really rationalizing myths and synthetic reasoning which were manufactured, post facto, to justify that unjustifiable spate of international looting which ransacked Africa, dehumanized a race, and mentally brutalized a people.

To begin with, there is no logical connection between negroes and slavery. Such a suggestion is patently false. Most people at one time or another were enslaved by other peoples, and a negro slavery was merely accidental. It was a purely economic phenomenon. From its cradle to its grave, it was determined by economic interests. Born out of economic circumstances it died, according to Eric Williams (who is the acknowledged authority here) not as the result of a belated humanitarian movement and convenient upsurge of Christian sentiment among people who wished to salvage moth-eaten consciences, but simply because as an economic institution, slavery had ceased to be profitable (Williams: Capitalism and Slavery-Negro in the Caribbean). The West Indies had become British by conquest. Cheap labor was sorely needed on sugar plantations to make them render the enormously high rates of return to finance the Industrial Revolution. The Indians, who were first exploited in the labor field, succumbed under the pressures of slave existence. Poor whites were brought down in droves from Western Europe under a system of glorified slavery called Indenture – some were kidnapped, some were tricked into coming, some were transported as convicts, while some sought political asylum. It was a motley array of people, often including the scum and off-scourings of the metropolitan power that provoked Benjamin Franklin to object to "this dumping upon the New World of the outcasts of the Old," an objection which bristles with contemporary significance. Somehow this brood proved unequal to the rigors of plantation life under a blazing tropical sun and was not forthcoming in sufficient quantities. So it was, with the failure of both experiments, that recourse was had to negroes of West Africa.

One of the most demoralizing myths conjured up by the apostles of slavery and which is enshrined in the heart of every true colonialist is that slavery removed us from a savage and nightmarish society marked by sheer barbarity, characterized by unbridled cannibalism and dominated by superstition. This is fatuous nonsense which flies in the face of historical facts and has been exposed by recent anthropological research and archaeological findings which testify to the high level of civilization that flourished in West Africa of the day. We may have barely heard some news which seeped through the colonial curtain of Timbuktu as a great center of learning, of the Benin Bronzes, of the splendor that was Ashanti, of the glory that was the parent kingdom of Ghana, evidence of societies which had attained an advanced plane of sophistication. And if some parts of Africa admittedly were no earthly paradise, neither were they some satanic community of depraved sub humans and degenerate souls. Far from. Yet we daily batten on the dross dished out about Africa by

European historians who have political – and economic – axes to grind. So indoctrinated were our slave forbears with the fallacious notion of a completely backward Africa that the Creole slaves looked down upon the African immigrant who in turn distrusted him and refused to make him privy to slave conspiracies. Herein lies one of the most baneful legacies of slavery, West Indians denouncing everything African and disclaiming their African heritage while stressing, even fabricating, their European derivation, considering themselves superior to the extent of their contact with the Whites, albeit the physical contact of the whip or the more insidious embraces of social indoctrination, cultural capitulation and economic strangulation; the African distrusting his West Indian brother and always suspicious of his "mongrel personality" and European outlook which rubbed off on him during slavery.

It is also a damning indictment on colonial education, which is an outgrowth of slave society, that arch-pirates and privateers such as John Hawkins who perpetrated that putrid traffic in human souls, have been inherited as our historical heroes. It is a fact, and we speak from personal experience here, that colonial children tend to identify themselves, as they were no doubt meant to, with the epic figures of the slave traders rather than with the black cargoes chained below the decks, poisoned during calms, and jettisoned during storms in that horrid trans-Atlantic trip known to us flippantly as the Middle Passage. On the other hand, one hears nothing of Toussaint L'Overture or the countless black heroes who braved heavy odds in vain attempts to liberate their people, nor of Marcus Garvey, who tried to clean out the stables that slavery left. Nor are stories properly recorded about the many militant negroes who committed suicide rather than live a life in abject servility. Which brings us round to exploding another slave myth about negro submissiveness and docility. In fact, negroes drowned themselves rather than submit, poisoned themselves with their entire families in a mood of utter defiance, while some others like the Bush Negroes of the Guianas or the Jamaican Maroons ran away and ensconced themselves in mountain fastnesses and jungle rather than yield to the regimen and overlordship of the plantations. And of course, some banded themselves into well-knit fighting units and plotted revolts and insurrections causing the widely-held belief that had the Abolition Bill been further delayed, emancipation would have been effected from below as was the case in Haiti.

Some folk are very fond of the claim that through the God-given institution of slavery the White man was able to discharge part of his burden in civilizing the backward negroes by "Christianizing" West Africans. Without venturing a comment on whether or not Christianity has been an unmixed blessing, or even a good thing in the circumstances, our own submission here is that there must be a thousand-and-one ways of saving people's souls without the sacrifice of their bodies, for there seems to be no necessary link between slavery and Christianity – or is there? C.L.R. James in his clinical analysis of the Haitian Revolution (C.L.R. James – Black Jacobins) relates the story of a slave ship's captain who, while awaiting the loading of his black cargo in a West African port composed the hymn "How sweet the name of Jesus sounds." And Queen Elizabeth was so pleased with the profits accruing from a Hawkin's trip that she offered her thanksgiving to God by granting Hawkins three ships for a repeat journey called "The Solomon," "The John the Baptist," and "The Jesus." Apart from the tremendous missionary work put in by the Moravians and Baptists and, to a lesser extent Methodists, Christianity was generally administered to the slave population in small grudging doses. So opposed was the general run of planters to the spread of Christianity with its twin revolutionary doctrine of the fatherhood of God and the common brotherhood of man that Bickell, an Anglican curate in Jamaica, based his advocacy on the acceptable ground that Christianity would make the slaves more tractable. (Cf. M.G. Smith – Social Structure in the British Caribbean about 1820) "The safety of the Whites demands that we keep the negroes in the most profound ignorance" was the cry of a planter of the day, a cry whose possible contemporary relevance must give us pause.

So far, we have attempted to examine critically some of the baseless intellectual props of slavery. We have exposed some of the more blatant historical imbalances which clutter this very vexed question and have revealed the system as the unblushing exploitation of people of color who were degraded by a conspiracy of historical distortions and systematic plan of myths fabricated by another race to camouflage a philosophy of naked greed. Now we hope to give a thumbnail sketch of the daily life of a slave as background study to other problems which our slave heritage has left us, particularly in the economic and social fields. We select the day-to-day life of a field slave in Cane Grove Estate, St. Vincent (Cameron: Evolution of the Negro, Vol. 11), which typifies the normal existence of the largest category of slaves.

Our slave rises as early as 3:00 or 4:00 a.m. His so-called home (the wattle-and-daub type which still disgraces our countryside but decorates tourist brochures) is some miles removed from the estate field where he must report for work at 5:00 a.m. The driver calls the slaves to work by blowing on a conch-shell or whistle. Roll call follows and late-comers are flogged with tamarind rods or a cart whip. The slaves work in rows and anyone who attempts to slow down the tempo of work is whipped. A favored slave, usually upgraded for news carrying, is the driver. The field slaves are all black. The lighter complexioned are the mechanics in the workshops or the domestic slaves. The free colored predominate as accountants and bookkeepers. Some even own a few slaves to whom they are excessively brutal in a vain effort to advertise their social inaccessibility. The attorneys and managers are normally poor whites, while the owners form an absentee interest wallowing in profits and living in style in the metropolis.

At 9:00 there is an half hour break for breakfast for such as had the time, energy and wherewithal to prepare. Work resumes at 9:30 without interruption until 12:00 when there is a break for lunch for two hours. But during this break, our field slaves have to gather grass which he must take home with him at the end of the day. It has been observed that during the dry season, this occupation often takes up the full two hours. Afternoon work is done from 2:00 to 7:00 p.m. i.e., until dark. When he reaches home the slave surrenders his grass to the overseer and is flogged or sent to the stocks for the night if it proves inadequate. This is the routine task of the field slave except that during crop time the work is intensified. Now the slave has to put in an additional three full night's work in the factory or a half-night daily for the week.

The slave owner is legally obliged to feed his slaves. In reality he issues two or three pounds of salt fish per slave per week (here is the origin of a dietary pattern devoid of nutritional value which persists to this day) . For the rest, the slave feeds himself on ground provisions grown on mountain land or over-cropped sugar land which his owner has parceled out to him. The produce from these lands belongs to the slave, who is permitted to sell it in the Sunday morning markets and keep the proceeds, thus effecting that "happy coalition of interests" by which Master is freed from an additional burden and slave is allowed a modicum of independence.

The slave master is also supposed to clothe his slaves. He does this by giving annually six yards of blue stuff, not inappropriately known as bamboo and six yards of brown. Children are allowed a small strip to tie around their waists. For bed clothing, the slave receives a blanket every four to five years. This is the sort of social and economic organization which has bequeathed us with more than our fair share of problems; economic, social and cultural.

In the economic sphere, a one-crop plantation economy is a child of slavery. It is a satellite economy which is externally oriented and derives its raison d'etre from forces outside the colony. No thought is given to the domestic situation, industrialization is strictly taboo and notions about crop diversification are considered outlandish. For the home market demands only raw materials, and the Estate is a jealous God. The result has been lopsided economic development, a gross maldistribution of wealth in favor of the plantocracy and the local import-export entrepreneurs, and a precarious economic life which is peculiarly sensitive to outside price fluctuations and allergic to external marketing conditions. And our balance-of-payments position is jeopardized by the fact that the slave mentality has convinced us that nothing produced locally can match imported stuff. We saw that the slaves were given mountain or over-cropped sugar lands on which to set up their vegetable gardens. This marks the birth of the hard working West Indian peasantry and exposes the lie of the inefficient peasant and lazy negro which have come down to us as legacies of slavery. Where peasant production is small, it is, more often than not, due to the fact that peasants have been given marginal lands unfit for sugar which are rocky, possess poor soils, lend themselves to erosion, or are over cropped. It is still a Vincentian practice for over cropped land, or cut down forest areas, to be converted into temporary "yam pieces" for the laborer who works them until they are "good enough" for the estate to resume possession. Still the industry and resource shown by the slaves in working the gardens whose profits belonged to them, has elicited the favorable comment of many an observer. But it stands to reason, save among people who have been entangled in their own web of sordid lies, that sweating on somebody's estate for somebody's profit is not exactly the best of incentives to work conscientiously. Even in those benighted days of slavery, British economist Adam Smith defined the problem lucidly: "a person, who can acquire no property, can have no other interest than to eat as much, and to labor as little, as possible."

Nowadays, praedial larceny is very commonplace on most Vincentian estates. It might be that such practice is implicit in plantations society and inheres in the very logic of the feudal relationships which for the most part still exist today. M.G. Smith has told us that the slaves, being chattels, considered themselves, by definition, incapable of theft. Just as a cow does not steal its master's grass which simply fattens it for its master's use, so a slave cannot steal from its master when he is himself the property of the said master. It is an internal displacement of property. Similarly, it would appear that laborers who are tied body and soul to an estate – from the estate come their wages, their pasturage rights, their wattle-and-daub, their privilege to gather wood, their "ham piece," all of which can be revoked just like that – feel free to plunder and rifle their master's holdings without much pricking of conscience. This is not excusing, this is simply understanding. And it is a problem which spills over into the field of industrial relations. Here one can see how that unbridgeable gap, set up between the haves and the have-nots, has repercussed. Suddenly aware of their collective strength and alive to the political possibilities, Trade Unions tend to be overly militant, even belligerent, in their object of bringing management to its knees and atoning for the wrongs of history (the whole Mount Bentinck episode is a case in point). On the other hand stands the intransigent employer who finds it distasteful to sit as an equal around a conference table with the upstart son of a slave who, as an ambitious leader of the workers, is bent in solving the load of personality problems which slavery has heaped on his head.

It is precisely in the area of social relations that the harsh wounds of slavery have left their deepest scars. Not only was the European class system superimposed on our society, but it was underpinned with racial overtones, as we saw when giving a graphic picture of social organization in the heyday of slavery. The society was pyramidal with the Whites perched at the apex of the hierarchy, the mulatto brown born of White slave masters and Black slave mothers gyrating in-between, and a teeming mass of frustrated black souls resting resignedly at the base. In short, it was a society differing in degree only from the one in which we live today. Then, as now, people were obsessed with skin color and shade. People would go to ridiculous lengths in retracing a family tree to see whether it can be established that a tear-drop of white blood flowed in their veins. Today it is the same; people are no longer Black, they are coffee-grown, they are not Negro, they are mixed, the African-slave past recedes into a misty background and the British connection assumes monstrous proportions. There was and is a negative correlation between power and influence, and pigmentation. In the scheme of things, the whiter, the richer and more powerful – the blacker, the poorer and weaker. Then, as now, but admittedly with less force and more subtlety now, job opportunities were related to skin color. As the sociologist would put it, slave society was rigidly stratified, with very limited vertical mobility between classes, approximating a caste system. Status placements were based on ascriptive criteria, that is to say, your birth consigned you to a ready-made niche in society from which the whole course of your life could be mapped and plotted.

Under such stultifying conditions prepared by slavery the response of the lower-class descendant of slaves has been one of near resignation. He accepts the White power structure and if he does not subscribe to White values, he at least respects them and sets them up as his ideal. Since he has been placed unreservedly at the lowest rung of the social ladder with little chance for promotion, he simply lets go and lives a happy-go-lucky life. The "demonstration effect" of the big banquets staged by his master in the estate house has taken a toll on his mental make-up and his immediate reaction to the first flush of wealth is to squander and have a good time. His sights are very narrow but he sets a high premium on white collar jobs and hopes that his children will steer clear of manual labor which still smacks of the stench of slavery. When he rises to a job like road-driver – the slave name is still maintained – or police officer, he lords it over his charges and governs with a rule of thumb. Whenever he attempted to cooperate and speak on behalf of unfortunate fellow slaves in the past, he was beaten and punished, and so he has learned assiduously to mind his own business and is callous and indifferent to the misery of his neighbors so long as it does not affect him.

The slaves were encouraged to live a life of casual unions. Christian marriage would have been disruptive of estate life insofar as it would have divided a loyalty which the estate demanded totally. Added to this, of course, is another handover from slavery that, shut out from the locus of power and positions of influence, promiscuous sex relations alone made a man feel that he had some worth. His ability to pick and choose, to keep or cast off, gave a man some sort of psychological compensation in a situation where all other avenues for self-expression were closed.

The middle class for their part perform a nice balancing act in an unreal state of "betweenity" flanked by a group they hoped they have left and another they hope they will reach. Among this class, intellectual mimicry, social affectation, and subscription to the shibboleths of Western cultured behavior, obtrude. There is inordinate aping of European behavior to curry favor, reminiscent of the domestic slave of whom Trollope caustically remarked, "burning to be a white man and a scholar, and puzzling himself with fine words." "Bleaching to be a White man...." would be nearer the point today. It is this class of "Afro Saxons" who, by and large, staff the Civil Service and teaching profession; the motorized salariat, M.G. Smith terms them. As in the days of slavery when a premium was set on the mechanical implementation of orders from above and promotion was based on tale bearing and acquiescence, so is this middle class type generally characterized by boot licking and sycophancy which frustrates the working of the Government bureaucratic machinery and paves the way for the indiscriminate use of political terror. For obvious reasons, consideration of skin color has been most marked in this group. Even plainly negro folk, by virtue of the mixing with the Whites in clubs and organizations, are counted as pass-for Whites, or Vincentian Whites, what a sociologist calls "Associational Whites." Kitchener's dictum that 'If you are not White you are considered Black' does not apply. Here members are often preoccupied with marrying lighter skinned persons so that they can "raise their color and have nice straight-hair children." It is these people too, who, tenacious of a precarious status and wishing to maintain a social distance from the so-called lower class, are most severe in their dealings with their less fortunate brethren. Domestic Servants come in for rough handling in the homes of our middle class, who are the spiritual descendants of the free-colored in slave society who were brutal and tyrannical slave masters.

These are our footnotes on slavery. We have been saddled with a myriad of problems which demand a veritable revolution in attitudes before they can be solved. We believe that we must make an effort to blur class lines and demolish color barriers to create a well-integrated, coherent society and overhaul a decrepit social system. To accomplish this, we must correct and place in proper perspective notions of our past which have helped to tarnish our image and affect our personality structure. A kindly slave owner, Monk Lewis, claimed that he administered disputes among his charges easily because they believed that "massa can do no wrong." We have to shout, with Eric Williams, that "Massa day done." And mean it. Most of us are trained in irresponsibility and won't know what to do with independence if we got it. We were never allowed to call the tune and must learn how to stand up, assume self-confidence, make decisions for ourselves and not be entrapped like the freed slaves who, after years of paternalism by patronizing owners, were maladjusted in their semi-free society and looked nostalgically upon the days of slavery. Given a proper historical sense of ourselves we may be able to assess our position, define goals, establish priorities, and move on. Slavery has done its mischief, but we must not allow it to generate a momentum of its own and poison our future. We call for an overdue mental emancipation to invest our physical liberation with some meaning. Probably an awareness of the problem is the first step towards a solution.

**Dr Kenneth John holds a Ph.D. in Political Science from Manchester University. He is a newspaper columnist and a practicing lawyer in St Vincent and the Grenadines.**

# 5 ON AFRO-WEST INDIAN THINKING

By Kerwyn L. Morris

(Taken from Flambeau, Number 4, April 1966)

Vincentians, like many other West Indians, suffer from a very deep-seated European orientation, an orientation that is historical in origin and reflects a negative relationship, a relationship that we do not want to be reminded of, a relationship between slave and master.

Such an orientation can do no good for us as Afro-West Indians. I say Afro-West Indians for that is what we are. We are a people basically of African stock whether we want to accept this or not. But it is no direct fault of ours that we, a black people, are European in our orientation. Our orientation is the product of slavery and the deliberate doings of those British imperialists who, in drawing up our education syllabuses refused to include any mention of great black West Indians like Toussaint L'Overture, Marcus Garvey, Sylvester Williams, George Padmore, and C.L.R. James, to name but a few. We were never told of these men, so that in our search for heroes as youngsters we found our men in imperialists like William the Conqueror, Benjamin Disraeli and Winston Churchill.

Further we were never told of the true history of the land whence we were brought – black Africa, our fatherland. We were never told that Black Africa was more civilized than Europe throughout history and we were robbed of the black pride that our forefathers brought with them when they arrived in chains. We were never told that it was as a result of contact with Europeans that the glorious path of African development was altered. We were never told that centuries before the Europeans discovered the world was round our fathers made their pilgrimages to Mecca crossing the Sahara Desert from the ancient empires of Ghana, Mali and Songhal in West Africa using the stars for guidance. We were never told of the black kings and queens whose armies defeated early European attempts to capture us. But instead, to facilitate and prolong our subservience and oppression to this day we were told that we were cannibals and savages. Had we been exposed to Garvey and had our parents been more attentive when he spoke at our library in Kingstown, they might have followed him up and learned from him that "when Europe was inhabited by a race of cannibals, a race of savages, naked man, heathens and pagans, Africa was peopled with a race of cultured black men, who were masters in art, science, and literature, cultured and refined." And as Garvey also said and which unadulterated anthropological history proves true,

> "out of cold Europe these white men came,
> From caves, dens, and holes without any fame,
> Eating their dead's flesh and sucking their blood,
> Relics of a Mediterranean flood."'

So our black fathers were once great and proud men but we shall never be as great or as proud of ourselves as they were of themselves until we learn to think independently. Until we learn to think as Afro-West Indians as we truly are and not as Euro-West Indians. As Garvey further said, "we have a beautiful history and we shall create another in the future that will astonish the world." West Indians need to discover their long lost black pride which was so systematically removed by the same people who have us in colonial bondage up to this day, so that there is not the remotest possibility of asserting one's West Indian personality while embracing a European orientation. The latter must be dispensed with.

There is in our midst an abundance of hypocrites and black Uncle Toms who very often cannot see any further than their noses. These are the most dangerous elements of our society and the greatest obstacles to change. The so-called middleclass or black bourgeoisie is their breeding ground. They flourish there. Lately these elements have been brandishing lip-service to West-Indianization yet they are found to be more European than the Europeans themselves. They make frequent trips to their "Mother Country," then stand aloft on the Swiss Alps next door and look down with disdain upon the mass of black humanity. They become white like the surrounding snow for a moment. For them the well-dressed West-Indian is one who chokes himself with a tie (the symbol of our necks) and suffocates in a jacket. To further express my disgust with this manner of dress and terms of reference, I shall quote a poet from French Guiana, Leon Damas who in his poem called "Balance Sheet' said:

> "I feel ridiculous
> in their shoes, in their dinner jackets,
> in their stiff shirts, their paper collars,
> with their monocles and their bowler hats.
> I feel ridiculous
> With my toes that were not made

To sweat from morning to evening,
In their swaddling clothes that weaken my limbs
And deprive my body of its beauty

The same reactionary elements because of their orientation and its accompanying shortcomings and petty-mindedness are thus rendered grossly incapable of recognizing the true and full value of a successful Afro-West Indian when they are presented with one. However, I ask those who are weathering the storm "to hold strain" for it would not be long before others return to join in the struggle against these black middle-class humbugs – the enemies of progress. Progress for them means the usage of foreign personnel in preference to nationals when nationals are available; the fools and idiots have never been taught to value anything of their own origin.

As the elections draw nigh there is talk of West Indianizing St. Vincent through the use of textbooks with a West Indian orientation. This may be adequate for those people of school age and those out of school who could actually be West-Indianized. But what about those who cannot read, how are they to be West-Indianized? It will have to be by action rather than by spoken or written word and I am afraid there is no halfway measure where action is concerned, for action knows no compromise. How can we talk to them of West-Indian orientation and at the same time leave the dry-rotten faded-out portraits of European Governors, queens and kings in our living rooms? How can we go to Victoria Park and present arms to the British National Anthem and still talk of West Indianization to these people? The very name of the park must be changed, the anthem must be discarded for it was never intended to save us from damnation by only the sovereign. Can't we see it calls only for our continued subjection – "long to reign over us?" Can't we see that this is inviting continued oppression and subservience? Imagine the sons and daughters of Britain's slaves singing "Rule Britannia....Britain never shall be slaves!" Are we out of our minds or something? Britain never shall be enslaved we lustily sing, while we are still held in colonial bondage by her. And we are proud to sing this for the reward of a heavy-bread and a hot sweet-drink? Poor us! Brass medals must be returned or refused or given to the "yeah-yeah" boys, and there must be concerted efforts aimed at dispensing with the Queen's Birthday Parade. The island must be renamed Hairoun, its original name. I strongly feel that it is only by methods such as these that mass mobilization and complete West Indianization can be achieved. Are we prepared to use these methods? West Indianization calls for positive action now rather than idle words.

To old colonial stooges, this stinks with disloyalty and disrespect, but they must know that the concept of loyalty was one of the tools that forged a success out of colonialism. The more loyal you are the more colonized and subservient you are. Are we content to remain colonized and subservient? No! There is thus a choice to be made. One cannot remain colonial minded and be truly West-Indianized at the same time, and since the choice is for the latter then the former must take its exit and the sooner the better. We can never assert our true selves under a colonial mentality. If we want to be true Afro-West Indians, then down with colonialism and all its symbols and stooges.

**Kerwyn Morris is a retired civil servant and was, for many years, Chief Fisheries Officer of St. Vincent. He presently resides in St. Vincent and the Grenadines.**

# 6 ISSUES IN THE WINDWARDS-JAMAICA BANANA WAR

By George Beckford

(Taken from Flambeau, Number 4, April 1966)

[Editor's Note: Below we reprint the major part of an article first published in Vol.2, No.1 of New World Quarterly, with which "Flambeau" is associated. We believe that the subject dealt with is of overriding topical interest, and we especially recommend it as imperative reading to all.]

The movement from colonialism to independence in the West Indies in recent years has been associated with internal conflict over one issue or another. There has hardly been a dull moment. The debate on the siting of the Federal capital, the Jamaican oil refinery issues, to federate or not to federate, and during the past year, the Windward-Jamaica banana conflict, are but a few outstanding examples. A clear exposition of the real issues involved in these conflicts is necessary in order to understand the dilemma of West Indian Society at this critical stage. The present paper attempts to analyze the most recent conflict in these terms.

Ever since the banana became a commodity of international trade in the late nineteenth century, Jamaica has been the chief West Indian exporter. Today the situation has changed, with the four Windward Islands of Dominica, St. Lucia, St. Vincent and Grenada together rivaling Jamaica for the top berth. All the islands depend almost exclusively on the British market for their banana exports. Export production in the Windwards expanded at a dramatic rate over the past ten years from about three million stems a year in 1956 to over ten million stems in 1964. And by the end of last year Windward supplies to the U.K were slightly greater than those from Jamaica. Unfortunately, the combined total of Jamaica and the Windwards exceeded the amount the market could absorb at price levels obtaining in recent years and the bottom fell out of the market. Prices fell sharply from 70.15 pounds a ton before mid-October to 63.15, then to 56.15 pounds by November and to a record low of 39.5 by December 28. Though prices have rallied since, they have generally remained below seasonal levels of recent years.

These developments have stimulated stormy debates between interested parties as well as between governments. The debates have provided some insight into the factors which create an impasse between

West Indian territories over this and other issues. First, the banana war clearly exposes the vulnerability of the territories to manipulation by outside interests when operating as separate units. Second, public discussions arising from the conflict reveal the consistent failure of the West Indian Press (insofar as THE DAILY GLEANER is typical) to analyze regional (and other) issues from the point of view of popular West Indian interests. Third, the conflict reveals the ambivalence of the "better off" units like Jamaica in their relations with the "less advanced" territories on the one hand, and the rest of the world on the other.

In the first place, it will be established that these recent developments in the banana trade have resulted mainly from a conflict between two private firms and that no real conflict of interest existed between banana growers in Jamaica and the Windwards. West Indian growers were caught as pawns in a game between the agents they selected to market their fruits.

The banana industry in the West Indies as a whole consists of numerous small independent growers and a few relatively large producers. Administratively, the industry in the Windward Islands is serviced by grower cooperative-type associations which contract with Geest Industries Ltd. for marketing all export fruit. Decision-making is simple, straightforward and relatively well representative of grower interests. And the associations have been able to secure good marketing arrangements from the agent.

The Jamaican industry, on the other hand, is serviced by an inefficient administrative superstructure consisting of the ABIGA, a growers' association, a statutory insurance scheme and the Banana Board, a statutory body which is the sole exporting agent. Recently, the inefficiencies were exposed by a team of foreign marketing consultants though they have been recognized by local observers for several years. The consultants, in fact, merely extended points made by the local Sharp Commission of 1958-59, as they themselves admitted in their report. For exporting fruit, the Banana Board contracts with Elders and Fyffes, a subsidiary of United Fruit Company, and Jamaica Banana Producers Association, a Jamaican grower enterprise; but the latter is allotted only a minor share of total exports. Consequently, it is not considered in the rest of the discussion in this section.

All West Indian growers have the same basic interest: to obtain the best possible prices for all the fruit they supply to the market. This no one will deny. A struggle between growers for market shares is out of line with this basic interest since it is clear that higher prices could be obtained through cooperation, not only in regulating market supplies but also in realizing shipping economies if cooperation were extended to joint shipment by West Indian growers themselves. The marketing agents, on the other hand, are each primarily concerned with earning the highest possible rate of profit. Each agent would be better able to achieve this if it had a monopoly on the market. Elders and Fyffes were, indeed, in such a position before the emergence of Geest Industries, and have therefore been seriously concerned with the rapid erosion of their controlling and dominant position. There is no question that they would be in a happier position with Van Geest entirely out of the market, but at worst they would be prepared to make an accommodation if only they could control the larger share of the market. The rapid growth of Van Geest, on the other hand, must surely have demonstrated to that firm the possibility that one day it might capture the whole market or at worst acquire control of the major share. There has as yet been no evidence that the two are prepared for a compromise market-sharing agreement. In the normal course of events, some form of market agreement would tend to emerge when competitive tactics (price cutting, etc.) have resulted in sustained losses by either or both firms.

The point at issue here, however, is that the basic interests of the two groups of West Indian growers are more in line with each other than they are with the private interests of the respective marketing agents. Yet it appears that each agent was able to manipulate the representatives of each group of growers to align with the individual agent, and thus create an artificial conflict between Windwards and Jamaican grower representatives.

Even before the first big price decline of mid-October, grower representatives from Jamaica and the Windwards had decided to meet and discuss "the orderly marketing of fruit in the U.K." The meeting had been scheduled for late October 1964. The Daily Gleaner of October 17, 1964, made the following statement in reporting on the forthcoming parley: "The Windwards have always accepted it (agreement on the regulation of supplies) in principle. But they make it clear that they wanted their share of supplies to the market to be on percentage. This the Banana Board (Jamaica) was never willing to concede."

The talks in Kingston began on October 22, and from the outset it was clear that the issue of market-sharing would be the focus of attention. The Daily Gleaner of October 23, reporting on the opening of the conference stated that, "One of the principal bases for arriving at agreement on not over flooding the market in the future will be the percentage of British demand which each territory is supplying at the time of agreement, informed sources at the Banana Building report."

The grower representatives met by themselves for the first two days. Prior to the conference they had invited their respective marketing agents to join the talks in the closing stages, ostensibly to inform them of whatever decisions the representatives made earlier. But after two days, the representatives could reach no agreement. Time posed no immediate problem. They had a weekend ahead during which time they could have a chance to consult with their Government, with others and with themselves informally in order to pave the way for a mutually satisfactory compromise. Instead, they took the traditional, easy, but disastrous alternative of asking "outside" interests to solve the problem for them. According to a Gleaner report of October 24: "No formula was agreed....Instead it was agreed that the 14 Windward Islands' representatives will consult Mr. N. Van Geest on Monday morning next for evolution of a satisfactory formula. At the same time, the Jamaican representatives....will consult with Elders and Fyffes and the Jamaica Banana Producers Association....(After that) the two sides will meet again to see if a mutually satisfactory arrangement can be made."

This time the "outside" arbitrators were the two private firms with vested interests in the final outcome - interests which, as indicated above, are somewhat out of line with those of the growers themselves and which remained irreconcilable in the particular situation. The nature of the case is undoubtedly clearer in retrospect but even at the time it should have been obvious to any serious observer that the difference could not be resolved by references to the two agents involved in a private struggle for market control. Indeed, this was the surest way to consolidate the impasse. Since there is no evidence that the representatives deliberately wanted the talks to fail, their course of action must be interpreted as reflecting complete ignorance of the real issues involved in the situation.

The same Gleaner report of October 24 stated that the reasons why no agreement had yet been reached were (1) that the Windward Islands would not bind themselves without prior Geest approval and (2) the problem of supply quota (i.e., the quantities of fruit to be marketed in future by Jamaica and the Windwards respectively). Jamaica wanted these to be based on 1963 shipments or on an average of the past three years, while the Windwards wanted the quotas to be based on shipments in the last quarter prior to the talks, July through September, 1964. Jamaica's proposals were basically preposterous. It would ensure that Jamaica, and Elder and Fyffes, would be continually assured of the major market share. And it made no concession to the fact that the Windwards' production was still expanding while that of Jamaica had been stable for some time.

The Windwards' proposal, on the other hand, involved concession on their part since in any realistic projection of supplies their share of the market in the July to September quarter would be smaller than would normally obtain in subsequent years. In fact, by December 1964 weekly arrivals in the U.K. from the Windwards exceeded Jamaica's supplies by 25 per cent. In refusing the Windwards' proposals the Jamaica representatives revealed a characteristic shortsightedness and poor judgment. Past experience should have guided them to accept the proposal. For they had once before had the chance to secure a more favorable share if only they had conceded the principle of market-sharing on the occasion when the Windwards had first suggested this as the basis for regulating supplies to the U.K. They should, by now, have realized that postponement would always favor the Windwards.

Jamaica's proposals would no doubt have been satisfactory for Elders and Fyffes since it assured them of a major market share which they would otherwise fail to achieve. And they would never accept the Windwards' proposal so long as the one put forward by Jamaica remained a possibility. On the other hand, neither proposal could reasonably have been expected to satisfy Van Geest whose position would improve over time without any agreement. It should have surprised no one when the talks broke down after each delegation consulted with its marketing agent on the question of appropriate market shares.

After the breakdown of the talks, the banana bureaucracy in Jamaica launched a hostile campaign against the Windward Islands. The policy of the Board in fact seemed to have been dictated more by the private interests of Elders and Fyffes than by the true interests of Jamaican growers, as the following considerations suggest. The Daily Gleaner of November 4 carried the headline: "Parley fails; Jamaica moves to counter Windwards' drive for 200,000 tons next year." The news item reported on a decision of the Banana Board to launch a "crash programme for bananas" aiming at "250,000 tons (from present 175,000) in 1965." In announcing this, a spokesman for the Board was reported to have said, "It would be plainly stupid for us, in such circumstances to stand by and allow the market in which we have always held sway to be dominated by those whom we must now regard, regretfully, as our direct competitors."
The Gleaner of November 21 further stated that the industry leaders in Jamaica were convinced that "the only way to avoid being pushed around was to have superior production to the Windwards."

As already suggested above, the primary interest of Jamaican and all West Indian growers must be to secure the best possible prices for the fruit they produce for export. It is clear, therefore, that a forced expansion programme would be detrimental to their interest since this would result in oversupply and lower prices for all growers. To the growers themselves, dominance in the market must be a minor consideration, especially if this can only be achieved through a loss in revenue.

More direct evidence that the Banana Board was being used by Elders and Fyffes to help solve the latter's market control problem – at the expense of West Indian growers – is provided by the following news item in The Gleaner of November 28, after prices had fallen to 49.15 pounds a ton with an oversupply of fruit: "Two top executives of Elders and Fyffes....flew into Kingston....to advise the Banana Board of the marketing position and to arrive at a policy line. It is understood that decision was taken to exercise none of the curbs on shipment of bananas which are usually done when colder conditions set in and only best quality fruit is sent forward. The reasoning behind this decision was that any such measure would only cause the Windward Islands to expand their position in the market. It is now official banana industry policy to surrender no ground in the U.K. banana market."

It is clear from this that the Banana Board had passed the initiative for decision making and policy formulation over to Elders and Fyffes. A Statutory Authority is supposed to be responsible for policy formulation within the framework of overall Government policy. If it cannot perform this function it should be dissolved. In this case the Board, it seems, was merely acting as an agent for implementing the policy decisions of its marketing agent, instead of the reverse! Ironically, these policy decisions were to the detriment of all West Indian growers. For as I indicated in Caribbean Quarterly in June 1964: "....it is clear that if the proposed expansion (in Jamaica) were to materialize, the only losers will be the growers themselves. The market will absorb the proposed increase in supply only at lower prices than would otherwise obtain; thus the British consumer will pay less for bananas, the marketing companies will earn more from the increased volume handled, and only the West Indian grower stands to lose."

By and large, the way in which industry leaders in the West Indies were exploited by private foreign interests (to the detriment of the growers they represent) is perhaps a reflection of the general bankruptcy of the whole leadership class in the West Indies. But of equal significance is the fact that the West Indies make themselves more vulnerable to this kind of self-destructive manipulation by outsiders when operating as separate units. For it is clear that if we were together as one unit, the scope for artificial conflicts of this type would be reduced.

More interesting days still lie ahead because Fyffes and United Fruit are aware of the limitations to expansion of production in Jamaica and are currently seeking another Commonwealth source of supplies to solve their market control problem. It now seems that British Guiana will be the choice for dupe since negotiations with British Honduras were terminated following Dr. Jagan's defeat in Guyana. Earlier plans for production in Guyana had been suspended because the company was uncertain of Jagan's political posture. In a few years, then, Jamaica and Guyana will be at each other's throat and the present honeymoon between the Banana Board and Fyffes will be over. The handwriting is on the wall for those who care to see.

Most of us are well aware of the functional limitations of the conventional West Indian press. The manner in which the Daily Gleaner participated in the banana debate is only one example of an everyday phenomenon. It was also bad enough that the representatives of the West Indian industry, particularly those in Jamaica, allowed themselves to be maneuvered by the private marketing firms. But perhaps the most disconcerting aspect of the entire debate is the fact that when the Jamaican Government formally entered the picture its spokesman, the Minister of Trade and industry, endorsed the Banana Board's policy, a policy which, as pointed out above, was really handed down by Elders and Fyffes and which was hardly in the true interest of Jamaican growers.

The following excerpt is taken from a policy statement by Mr. Lightbourne, Jamaica's Trade Minister, on his return from Britain where he had talks with Jamaica's agents on the island's banana trade there: "It is essential at this time that we continue to sell all we can to Britain, because if we do not the Windwards will flood the market with their surplus production....we must not allow the Windwards to take over from us in a market that is traditionally ours."

It appears that Mr. Lightbourne, like the Board, allowed himself to be bamboozled by Elders and Fyffes who no doubt seduced him with the argument of traditional Jamaican dominance, as if this could in any way increase export earnings and bring more incomes to Jamaican banana growers. On the contrary, since dominance would mean oversupply on the market it could only be secured through lower prices to growers. All along, Fyffes was playing on Jamaica's characteristic insularity and petty nationalism which blinded not only the Banana Board and the Gleaner, but the Jamaican Government as well. None of these could see the real issues involved even though they were obvious enough, as New World Fortnightly, the Time and Economist were able to demonstrate.

The constitutional independence of Jamaica appears farcical in the particular context. For the Government had the appearance of a puppet for the ventriloquist, Elders and Fyffes. Whereas the chain of policy formulation and decision making should normally be from the Government to the Statutory Authority then to the Authority's marketing agent for implementation, the actual linkage in this case was backward. A private firm called the tune and all Jamaica jumped.

The Minister's policy statement, detrimental as it was to the growers themselves, also shows an unsympathetic approach to a problem crucial to the Windwards' economies and at the same time peripheral to the economy of Jamaica. If an opportunity ever presented itself for Jamaica to restore the confidence of the smaller West Indian territories after its decision to withdraw from the Federation, this was it. Bananas account for less than 7 per cent of Jamaica's total exports. But over 70 per cent of Windwards' exports are derived from bananas. (In St. Lucia alone, the share is now about 85%). Concessions to the Windwards would hardly affect Jamaica's export earnings and would perhaps increase revenue to the grower, through higher prices. It would be a demonstration of regional awareness on the part of Jamaica and a show of concern for the less developed smaller territories – all at no monetary cost. Instead, the totally irrelevant argument of a traditional place in the market was the main policy consideration.

It really should not be surprising that the Jamaica Government has shown no concern with the development problems of the "less advanced" West Indian islands, with which it was once constitutionally associated. After all, even inside Jamaica itself successive administrations have shown little real concern with closing the income and status gaps existing within the country. And, as the saying toes, charity begins at home! Yet the same governments have consistently exhorted the more advanced countries to help close the gap between rich and poor countries, classifying themselves conveniently in the latter group in order to obtain concessions and handouts. Jamaica makes the case to the United States, for example, that the latter should diversify away from light manufacturing, such as textiles, in favor of countries like Jamaica. What then of Jamaica's position vis-à-vis the Windward Islands?

**Dr. George Beckford was Professor of Economics at the University of the West Indies in Mona, Jamaica. His specialty was Agricultural Economics. He died in 1990.**

# 7 GARY SOBERS AND THE BRISBANE REVOLUTION

By Woodville Marshall

(Taken from Flambeau, No. 5, July 1966)

[EDITOR'S NOTE: By the time that this issue of "Flambeau" reaches our readers, the West Indies will be smack in the middle of yet another "great Test Series against England". In "The Brisbane Revolution," Woodville Marshall tells us all about recent cricket development in the West Indies and much more. The article, reprinted from the 1965 Dead Season issue of New World Quarterly, provides a rare treat for anyone with more than a sports-page acquaintance with the game, as well as produces a fascinating study for social commentators. This article is a "must" for all those who take their cricket or their society seriously, and want to probe beneath surface appearances to get to the deeper meaning of things.]

The "Brisbane revolution" is a limited revolution. What has happened to cricket since 1960-61 might be of some significance for the West Indian communities and for a section of West Indian cricket, but it means little to the game in general. The West Indians (and Australians) were credited with having started a great cricket revival in 1960-61 which was continued in England in 1963. Throughout this period (1960-65) the West Indians not only played the "bright" and "exciting" cricket for which they have become famous, but they also played it with unprecedented distinction and success. They managed to produce clear-cut results in sixteen of their twenty Test matches; they won eleven of their Test matches and three of their four Test series; and wherever they have played they involved most of the spectators deeply in the game and in its outcome. Johnny Moyes' comment on the performance of the West Indians during their tour to Australia in 1960-61 is illuminating. "The impact they made on cricket in Australia was amazing," he wrote. "They turned the world upside down....they gave the genuine cricket lover a thrill he had not felt for a quarter of a century." Equally significant is Alan Ross' tribute to the West Indians after the tour of England in 1963, "Enriching the common idiom of the game, they restored to it not only spontaneity, but style." This was and is the "revolution" in action.

But few, if any, of the major cricketing countries have attempted in the last five years to catch the sparkle of the West Indies performance and example. Most Test matches (and nearly all English county matches) continue to be tedious games of attrition with clear-cut results laboriously achieved, if achieved at all. Mediocre seam bowlers on inadequately prepared pitches dominate the game and spinners, particularly leg-spinners, are a luxury few teams can afford. (Even in the popular English one-day Knock Out (KO) matches, the spinners are often dropped from the county teams for these matches, and if they are selected they are used either as batsmen or as slow-medium seam bowlers.) The batsmen, often mediocre in quality, appear even more pedestrian in performance because they fear to venture more. They too are infected by the seam bowling and "professional" psychology. Consequently, a definite result to a game (particularly a Test match) is an exception and a relief and sometimes a national disaster. The spectator seems to have been forgotten although he is the necessary witness of this exercise in futility. All captains and managers of touring teams assiduously pay lip service to the god of "brighter cricket;" yet when not playing the West Indies, neither India, Pakistan, New Zealand, South Africa, England nor Australia manage to entertain the long suffering spectator or to terminate the depressingly long series of drawn games. Recently, Ken Barrington, the most successful English batsman in the past six years, spent over seven hours in compiling a century against a weak New Zealand bowling attack apparently without being reprimanded by his captain. The English selectors, in a sudden and startling fit of memory of the bright promises easily given and callously tarnished, dropped Barrington "more in sorrow than in anger" for his pointless vigil. But if the selectors intended to be consistent or to be taken seriously, they should also have dropped the captain for the following match. In addition, one wonders whether the selectors' new-found solicitude for the game and for the spectators would have operated at all if England had been involved in a Test Series against Australia, the West Indies or South Africa. In short, the "revolution" as far as the game in general is concerned, remains an empty, pious promise made at the start of every cricket season and of every Test series which is occasionally and accidentally redeemed by the presence and genius of personalities like Dexter, Burge, R.G. Pollock or Trueman.

The "revolution," then, is mainly a West Indian phenomenon. The change in West Indian cricket has been profound. The nature and extent of this change can be seen most easily in the success of West Indian cricket during the last five years. There has been more to this success than "brightness" and "exotic" flavor. In the first place, the West Indies has finally emerged as the leading cricket country. Ever since the tour to Australia in 1960-61 when, as Jack Fingleton says, the West Indies team won the "gold" of defeat but lost the silver of victory, the West Indies, in successively outclassing India, England and Australia, has demonstrated clearly that the potential for greatness which West Indian cricketers have always possessed in plenty but which has never been consistently realized has at last been translated into the world supremacy of the West Indies cricket team. The West Indies team has reached its pre-eminent position, not because the other cricketing countries have grown weaker, but because the West Indies has become stronger. It is true that the West Indies team has managed to retain a nucleus of five or six brilliant players throughout the last five years, but the situation is no different from that of the 1950's. Yet no real comparison can be made between the performances of the West Indies teams of these two periods. It would seem that in the most recent period, unlike the earlier period, the West Indies team has become stronger mainly because the brilliant talents of the individual players are being fully exploited in the interest of the team.

Secondly, the West Indies, in the process of securing its cricket supremacy, has shown how a spectator sport in danger of death by tedium and spectators' lack of interest might be revitalized. The West Indian cricketers always seem aware of the responsibility of cricket and cricketers: the game exists to give pleasure and entertainment to players and spectators. Foreign commentators and spectators have been most impressed by this aspect of West Indian cricket. Johnny Moyes, an Australian Commentator on the West Indies visit to Australia in 1960-61, remarked that the crowds were brought back to the Australian cricket grounds because the West Indians played cricket both "as a game and an entertainment;" and the Australians' tumultuous and sentimental "au revoir" to the West Indian team, as it left Melbourne in 1961, was doubtless the most thunderous demand for an encore ever heard or witnessed. George Duckworth, reviewing the West Indies visit to England in 1963, declared in Wisden that the West Indians "sparkling batting, bowling and fielding," forced "the whole nation to follow the progress of the Tests." Even Christine Keeler and Profumo were occasionally forgotten in that damp, gossip-laden summer when the West Indians entertained at Lords or the Oval. Alan Ross provides the most graceful comment on the impact of West Indian cricket on the English cricket public: "The West Indies were unquestionably the most entertaining side to have played in England in thirty years, and though they had, on green wickets, their weaknesses, that was at least part of their charm. They were never stingy with their gifts, they followed their individual stars, and they provided, even as they gained, enormous pleasure." It is not surprising, therefore, that the M.C.C. should have altered its timetable of cricket tours so as to enable the English cricket public to see the West Indians again in 1966 rather than in 1970. (The only unfortunate consequence of this new arrangement is that the English spectators will see West Indians twice before the West Indian cricket public sees the English team.)

Thirdly, the achievements of the West Indies cricket team have been marked by a new mental toughness, a sense of team unity and a resilience under pressure seldom observed in the past. This new quality in the performance of the team is the most significant new departure. The West Indies has often produced brilliant individual performers like Headley, Constantine, Chandler and John, but it has never produced until now a consistently outstanding team. Even in the fifties when the West Indies could call on the Ws, Stollmeyer, Ramadhin and Valentine, Christiani, Gomez and Marshall, the success of the team never came near to matching the accumulated brilliance of the individual performers. This absence of team spirit and unity has provoked much comment in the past from foreign commentators in particular, who might have consciously exaggerated the defect. To them, West Indian Cricketers were primarily a variant on the Black and White minstrels; they were a "band of entertainers," volatile, unpredictable, excitable and exciting, almost childlike. Johnny Moyes thought that when the West Indies team arrived in Australia in 1960 it had "no idea of teamwork; no sense of cohesion." Despite the triumphant reputation of this criticism by West Indian performances in most of the subsequent Test matches, Phil Tressider, an Australian correspondent of the Playfair Cricket monthly, could still trot out the hoary myth for inspection at the start of the recent Test Series between West Indies and Australia. He said then that the Australians' "team spirit, resolve and competence," might well triumph over the "most talented lineup of individuals."

But despite the probable exaggeration in all these comments, it is fair to say that West Indian teams, until recently, were hopelessly divided mainly along social and insular lines. This partly explains the failure of the teams of the fifties which contained our greatest ever galaxy of stars. Frank Worrell, the most brilliant of these, found the teams so full of "factions" that he could write of joining the "neutralist ranks" during the 1951-52 tour to Australia. (The neutralists were those who refused to offer advice to John Goddard who profited greatly in England in 1950 from the availability of such advice.) Throughout the 'fifties West Indian cricket suffered from inept captaincy and slipshod administration; but, in addition, discord was bred in the teams by personal and insular rivalries and loyalties and by the self-centered determination of established players to protect their reputations and positions against the claims of the younger, promising members of the teams.

But since 1960-61, West Indian teams have found a sense of purposeful unity. This is due, in part, to the shrewd and sensible leadership of Frank Worrell. Worrell had always been aware of the flaring deficiencies of the West Indian teams; and after the humiliating experience of the 1957 tour to England, he realized that it was "clearly time for a new policy" which could exploit fully the potential of all players. His new policy, which he implemented on succeeding to the captaincy, was to give each touring player a fair opportunity to qualify for selection of the Test team; "there was no reason," he writes, "for us to establish a first team within the team for what were considered important matches, thereby giving the less experienced players an inferiority complex." The results of this wise decision and direction were and are dramatic. Johnny Moyes had to eat his words (and one hopes that Tressider will publicly follow suit) and he did this very cheerfully. By the time the first Test started at Bribane, Moyes realized that there were "no divisions" in the West Indies team; "the spare parts came together to form a machine which could function efficiently under the guidance of a master mechanic."

Events at Brisbane (1960), at Lords and the Oval (1963) and at Bridgetown (1965) point to the continuous presence of the new maturity and team spirit. In all of these instances, the West Indies Test Team not only recovered from apparently weak positions to draw or win, but also gained great glory for itself by the manner of recovery. In all these instances, there were brilliant individual performances, but the glory was won because the effort was as much a team effort as that of a Hall, a Kanhai, a Hunte or a Nurse. Clearly then, what was initiated with Worrell has not changed. The West Indies has won its way to cricket supremacy by a wise cultivation of the advantages of team unity. This was started with Worrell, and Sobers has already shown that he can exploit and perhaps add to the legacy of team work left him by Worrell.

A new quality of leadership is thus obviously part of the explanation of the recent success of West Indies cricket. But this can hardly be the full explanation of the recent conquest of heights which have often been tantalizingly missed in the past. Further questions must be asked and answered before the new situation becomes wholly comprehensible. How did the new leadership – the Worrell-Sobers axis – reach its position of leadership? Can it maintain its position? Why have the members of the team responded so quickly and wholeheartedly to the new policies of team selection and to the leadership of the captains? Is the new team unity wholly the creation of sane captaincy? If it is possible to offer an adequate answer to some of these questions then it will be possible both to talk rationally of a "revolution" and to expect the continued success of West Indian cricket. Some sort of answer is suggested by the presence and operation of certain socio-political factors.

Three interacting agencies of pressure might be isolated. In the first place, political events in the area during the last twenty years have affected the situation. The West Indies has been moving fitfully towards the appearance of democracy and this is reflected in trade union activity, universal adult suffrage, apparently mass-based political parties. The people – the underprivileged sector – are on the scene of politics even if they do not dominate it. It has become increasingly necessary for the social and political elite groups to offer the people the shadow, if not the substance, of power. Consequently, there has been a proliferation of symbols designed to damp down the frustrations of centuries. If politicians must appear to act for the people and to seem, of the people, so, too, must the administrators of cricket which has a following perhaps larger and more devoted than any political party. In some ways, cricket has in the past anticipated social change in the West Indies; but since the recent political events seem to have outdistanced it, pressure is being applied on the administration of the game to reflect the changing political situation.

Secondly, there is the impressive and, to some extent, embarrassingly long list of achievements by numerous cricketers from the underprivileged sector of the community. There were (and are) the cricketers who did not possess a background in the aristocracy or in the upper reaches of the mercantile community; they had their origins in the colored and Negro lower-middle and lower classes. The contribution that cricketers like George John, Wilton St. Hill, Learie Constantine, George Headley, Herman Griffith, Derek Sealey, Everton Weekes, Frank Worrell, Sonny Ramadhin and Alfred Valentine made to West Indian cricket during the last forty years needs no special emphasis. These men were West Indian cricket – both locally and internationally. At the present time, West Indian cricket rests mainly on the shoulders of the same class of individuals – Sobers, Hunte, Kanhai and Butcher, Griffith, Hall and Gibbs. Yet West Indian cricket administration and leadership positions have been (and to some extent still are) dominated by a small white and "high brown" oligarchy which rules at Kingston Cricket Club, Queen's Park, Pickwick and G.C.C. and barely acknowledges the claims to leadership of the members of Melbourne, Maple, Spartan and D.C.C. and completely ignores those of the members of Boys' Town, Shannon, the

Barbados Cricket League and Transport. This does not, by any means, exhaust the intricate social complexities of cricket; there are black and lower class clubs, black and colored professional middle class clubs, off-white and poor white clubs, wealthy white clubs. There is also a degree of social mobility: a black player from a lower status club can enjoy a limited climb upwards as his success at cricket alters his social status. But this is the main outline of the reflection of the social situation in the game: the lower status clubs provide the bulk of players for the West Indian teams and most of the brilliant individual performers while the higher status clubs provide the captains and most of the personnel of the Cricket Associations and Boards of Control. But, in the context of an apparently changing political scene, this situation would and did come in for open criticism.

The third agency of pressure then is the criticism which was mainly articulated by C.L.R. James. James has recognized the degree to which West Indian social history is involved with cricket and the great extent to which native cultural expression (particularly among West Indian males) exists only through participation in this game. He has recognized, too, that the administration and leadership of a game which is of such crucial social and cultural importance should reflect the existence of the eminent social forces which give it its importance. James has expressed all this and much more in his "Beyond a Boundary"; and it was James again who, in many articles in the Nation during 1959 and 1960 argued powerfully for reform of cricket's administration, for the reinstatement of Gilchrist and for the appointment of Worrell as West Indies captain. James was the first apostle of the revolution. Operating as he did simultaneously in a mass political party context, James articulated and directed a popular resentment which was always likely to erupt in violence and which did erupt into violence at Bourda in 1954 and at Queen's Park in 1960. He said publicly (and in a political party's newspaper) what should have been said for more than a generation; he wrote what, because of an out-worn Boy Scout and Public School morality, had only been muttered on verandahs and in bars. It was James principally who had caused popular pressure to be applied with some success to the oligarchic structure of West Indian cricket administration.

The result of this combined pressure has been a more complete social breakthrough in terms of fuller popular participation in cricket on the field. For a long time now it has been possible for any talented cricketer to win selection on West Indian teams, but now it would seem that all members of the West Indian communities as well as all the cricketers themselves can at last feel a sense of identification with the game because nearly all the socio-economic barriers to vertical mobility by players inside the game have been removed. One captain has been selected on the basis of his merit as a player. This innovation seems to have released the full energies and abilities of most of the cricketers; they are now performing for themselves as well as for the community because they have realized that a small, narrow-minded, self perpetuating social oligarchy no longer completely dominates their cricket world. All of them have equal opportunity to win selection on the Test team; any one of them could become its captain.

    This represents a complete break (one hopes) with a past in which West Indian cricket administrators and selectors, in an attempt to circumvent the considerable claims of George Headley to the captaincy of the West Indies team in 1947, could create a farcical situation by appointing, before the series started, Goddard, Stollmeyer and Headley as the captains for the four matches! Similar examples abound: a mediocre cricketer like Dennis Atkinson was appointed captain in 1955; an aging John Goddard was resurrected after his failures in Australia in 1952-53 to lead the team to England in 1957; a sadly inexperienced Cambridge Blue, F.C. Alexander, was predictably appointed captain between 1958 and 1960. In all these instances, the selectors ignored the considerable claims of Worrell and the lesser but still weighty claims of Walcott and Weekes; the traditional leadership and dominance of Kingston Cricket Club and Pickwick-Wanderers were maintained. In most of these instances, the remarkable potential possessed by the individual members of West Indian teams was frittered away in inept captaincy and by an absence of team spirit; and throughout the fifties, such a policy repeated its rewards in the embarrassment and deep humiliation of West Indian cricket – both at home and abroad.

    West Indian achievement in cricket over the last five years reflects the existence of a new situation. This is not to suggest that the presence of certain social or political factors can ensure success in any game. A game is by its very nature non-deterministic. Chance and the individual temperament affect performance and outcome to a significant degree. But outside these imponderables, there are areas which can be developed by the application of skill in leadership, by rationality in team selection, and by self-conscious attempt to create team spirit. In these ways, success in the game might not be ensured, but the chances of defeat and humiliation are reduced. What is new in West Indies cricket is that neither the team nor the West Indies cricket public expects defeat or frequent, total and inexplicable collapses – and, partly as a result, neither of these has occurred with any regularity in the last five years.

Worrell's belated appointment as captain in 1960 marks, then, the start of the "revolution;" and Sobers' succession to the leadership seems to consolidate it, for, as C.L.R. James has written, he is "the first unambiguously native West Indian who has arrived at the exalted position." He is the most complete of cricketers; he is the most professional of cricketers. Sobers is in the long tradition of underprivileged West Indians who raised their own social status by conspicuous excellence at Cricket. Therefore, it is particularly fitting that he should be available both to help in the consolidation and extension of the local limited revolution and to carry its exciting doctrines outside the West Indies. Sobers has neither inherited nor acquired any of the high-status social and economic advantages – no rich father, no high color, no good school, no university degree. His total assets have been his ability at games, particularly at cricket, and his determination to rise to the top of this game. He has set himself over the last ten years to master most departments of the game. Starting his international career in 1954 as an orthodox slow left-arm bowler who could also bat, he developed his batting until he became the world's leading batsman in 1960. In the meantime, he decided to experiment with 'chinamen' and googlies, and later on he developed his talents as a medium-fast swing bowler. Today, his mastery of all these arts is plain to see: a compelling batsman, a successful and dangerous swing and seam bowler, a deceptive spinner, a magnificent slip fieldsman who is peerless at leg-slip. He has played cricket for a living and for pleasure in most parts of the world; from the time of his early successes in the Barbados Cricket League when he was only fourteen, to his records in the Australia Sheffield Shield in 1963 and 1964 to his captaincy of the West Indies cricket team; cricket has been his life.

But he is no mere journeyman, no jack of all trades. He is no Barrington of dull utilitarian competence; he is both a professional and a genius. When he moves in the field or on to the field, the whole game sits up and takes notice: the master has arrived and, particularly when he is batting, every moment becomes charged with expectancy. He possesses, as Neville Cardus has discovered, "a rare store of genius" which has perhaps been most fully displayed since he has become captain of the West Indies team. E.W. Swanton caught a glimpse of that genius during the recent Test match at Bourda. He writes in "The Cricketer": "One's abiding memory of this game will be of Sobers – batting, with an almost arrogant freedom, bowling fast, bowling chinamen, bowling orthodox slow, picking up slick catches near the bat, giving his side in the field a general example that they vied with one another in following, directing the whole effort, and all the time looking every inch what he is, the most marvelous natural cricketer in the world." One can only add to this that his considerable technical skills, his flair for the whole game and his ability to take and hold command, make him better equipped and qualified than any other cricketer to keep West Indian cricket supreme and to throw down the challenge (in the title and content of his recent book) "Cricket Advance!" The only regret is a selfish one. The art of batting has lost a rare adornment if Sobers has decided, as he seems to have decided, to call himself an all-rounder and bat at number six. Perhaps such a decision means that Sobers becomes more valuable to the team; but we will all miss the aesthetic thrill of his easy arrogant dominance of the bowlers.

Finally, one must note the limited nature of the local revolution. Cricket needs further democratization in the West Indies. Players (and spectators) might feel more fully identified with what happens on the field, but the game off the field is still largely dominated by the old narrow oligarchies. If West Indian cricket is to realize its full potential, the administration of the game must be reformed so as to ensure that the wisest cricket heads share in the administration of the game and that all sectors of the community receive the material and psychological encouragement to put their fullest into the game. Our administration has never served West Indian cricket well. The errors committed in selection of teams and captains have been compounded by a refusal to ensure the provision of the best possible facilities for the development of the game in rural areas and in the smaller cricketing territories. The administration has shown an embarrassing tendency to put accumulation of cash before general improvement of the game. Most recently, the West Indian cricket Board of Control's criminal short-sightedness nearly jeopardized the chances of our team's success against Australia. No provision was made for a series of team practice matches before the arrival of the Australians even though the members of the West Indian team had not played together for eighteen months. It is clear, therefore, that until the power of the oligarchical group in the administration of West Indian cricket is completely broken, the revolution cannot be regarded as complete. The enemy might have been driven from the field, but vigilance must still be exercised by social commentators and by the cricketers themselves to ensure that he does not merely retreat, in fairly good order, into the fastnesses of the committee rooms and exclusive clubs.

For this reason, Sobers and the other young cricketers now rising to the fore of West Indian cricket have a special responsibility in the game and in the community. The enemy is wily; he might choke off the opposition in an elitist embrace by granting some of its leaders limited access to higher ranks and exclusive clubs. This will amount to subversion. The maneuver can only be countered by a thoroughgoing public discussion of the social issues involved in the game and mainly by a consistent refusal by our leading players from the underprivileged sector of the community to accept the pressing invitations to join and play for Queen's Park or Kingston Cricket Club. It must be admitted that some sacrifice of the social amenities in the first class game might have to be endured with such a refusal; but it would appear that such a sacrifice is not too great a one to make in order to deny the tottering oligarchic structure the new props it needs to prevent it from falling. Frank Worrell's decision to play for Boys' Town on his return from England was apparently made in this spirit; and all those other cricketers who have enjoyed social and material success as a result of their outstanding merit as cricketers, should recognize the absolute necessity for taking and abiding by similar tough decisions.

**Dr Woodville Marshall is Professor Emeritus of History at the Cave Hill campus of the University of the West Indies in Barbados. He presently resides in Barbados.**

## 8 INDEPENDENCE, UNITY AND NON-ALIGNMENT – THE ONLY HOPE

By Kerwyn Morris

(Taken from Flambeau, Number 5, July 1966)

The policy of non-alignment is quite common among the so-called "developing areas" of the world – those areas that are shaking off, once and for all, the yokes of western colonialism and imperialism.

The smaller English-speaking islands of the Caribbean still under these yokes, have either now accepted or had forced down their throats a new constitution that paves the way for an extended period of colonial servitude to Britain. The British Labor Party Government of Harold Wilson is rapidly proving itself to be more of a nuisance and a betrayal to the colonial peoples than the Conservative Party. But however fraudulent the constitution may be, it is necessary that we understand what colonialism and imperialism are, so that we may have a true concept of where we stood in history, where we stand now, and where we are headed for, if we allow these evil practices to continue. Our brothers in Africa, Asia and Latin America are today still facing problems left by those iniquitous practices and it is only fitting that we identify ourselves with these peoples and see how they are solving their problems. The colonial and imperial powers will never solve them for us and it is naïve for us to depend on them to do so. We have to take the reigns of full and responsible government into our hands – **including foreign affairs**.

Colonialism is the practice of holding peoples in subjection for the purpose of exploiting them and their natural resources without due regard for the interests of these peoples. The interests of the "mother country" come first – in fact, those are the only interests that exist in a colonial relationship. Colonizing countries are the only mothers that suck from their young instead of giving suckle to their young. These colonized and muzzled peoples have no sovereignty of their own and are forced, very often with firearms, to acknowledge the complete sovereignty of the colonizing power. The resulting conditions always leave the majority of these peoples existing at subhuman standards, and very often it is only by violence that the sucking mothers and leeches can be shaken off. It happened in Haiti, it happened in Algeria, it happened in India and it is now happening in Viet Nam. As a people having a common colonial past, we should throw our full support behind the Buddhists and the Liberation

Front in their bitter struggle against American imperialism. It was against these conditions that men like Chaka, Toussaint and Chatoyer fought, yet they were recorded as warriors and enemies. What a sad commentary on history. But history and time were on their sides and will always be on the side of those struggling for meaningful progress. The march of history and a peoples' struggle for liberation can never be stopped by firearms.

Imperialism is the practice often, though not always by the same colonizing powers, of maintaining economic and administrative control over former colonies that have been "granted" independence. This practice is rampant throughout Africa. This is what Nkrumah was fighting against! This is what was at the back of the "Guinean experience" with France when Guinea voted out of the French commune! This is what the Euro-American air-lift of mercenaries into the Congo was about! This is what the American invasion into the Dominican Republic was about (under the pretext of saving the lives of American nationals), and such an invasion is exactly what will take place when progressive governments come to power in the islands of the Caribbean and try to strangle imperialism. For progress to be made, imperialism must be stamped out for they are both incompatible, and the independent countries that fail to eradicate it can boast only of paper independence – an empty boast.

In January this year, the victims of colonialism and imperialism held a mammoth Tricontinental Conference in Havana called the First Solidarity Conference of the People of Asia, Africa and Latin America and there were 83 delegates from 82 countries of Asia, Africa and Latin America present. It is too sad that we did not see it fit to send a delegation, but instead joined the imperialists in dubbing it a "hate conference." It is quite time that we give our full and unflinching support to our brothers who have suffered under the same evil practices and join them in solidarity against the common enemy.

In order that the Caribbean may pursue a policy of non-alignment, two fundamental prerequisites must be met. One is independence and the other Caribbean unity. By independence is meant not just the acquisition of a flag and the chanting of a new national anthem, for real and meaningful independence is more than this. It means the ability to pursue certain economic and political policies unfettered by previous obligations made over our heads by the colonial warlords and their associates, without regard for our interests. It means the ability to speak frankly without fear or favor on issues of world importance. It means the ability to condemn American action in Viet Nam, Africa, Latin America, and the Caribbean. It means the ability to place the interests of the Caribbean above the interests of Europe and North America. In short, it means the exercise of our freedom and sovereignty to their fullest in every respect for it must be remembered that only a free people can shape their destiny. The type of independence advocated here is not insular but rather a sort of federated independent group as a unit. The true and ultimate independence of the Caribbean can come only after Caribbean unity.

The other prerequisite, that of Caribbean Unity, means the political and economic integration of every single piece of land mass in the Caribbean, regardless of its political and economic systems. We all have common origins, problems, histories, aspirations and enemies; and division in the face of the enemies of progress is not something to be desired.

The Caribbean, it must be borne in mind, was not divided to suit our interests but rather those of Europe and it was no accident each time we were kicked around like a political football. The time is long past due when we must turn our attention to the interests of the Caribbean and when we do this, we discover that nothing short of total integration is the answer. But as we attempt this, we encounter the problems of a divided people on the one hand, and the menacing presence of American imperialism on the other. Thus if ever the islands of the Caribbean intend to seek unity among themselves, then we must be prepared to do battle on both fronts simultaneously. We must confront the problems that stem from our colonial legacy, and launch a militant and relentless offensive on the forces of imperialism. As a divided Caribbean, we can never hope to free ourselves from American harassment in all its varied forms, but as a United Caribbean we may at least be able to keep the enemy at bay.

It may be argued that our geographical location makes a policy of non-alignment impossible, but is Algeria far from France, is Yugoslavia far from USSR, or is Indonesia far from Australia?

Non-alignment does not mean a negative attitude or indifference towards world events but rather the taking of an independent stand on issues without any obligation to either power bloc. This policy, combined with positive neutrality, indicates that in so doing, we would be making use of the benefits of the experiences of certain past events, comparing these with present day realities, and seeking to avoid any unpleasant event that the enemies of progress and world peace may have in store for us.

It is only by pursuing a policy of non-alignment that peaceful co-existence can have any meaning. If we believe in peaceful co-existence, then we have to be non-aligned, for alignment means the denial of harmonious relations between all mankind. Peaceful co-existence, which should be our guideline in international relations, does not allow us to dis-acknowledge the existence of any sovereign state. We cannot, like some nations, talk of peaceful co-existence and refuse to recognize 650 million Chinese or 7 million Cubans – our neighbors. This is the Western type of co-existence which, as we can clearly see, is co-existence only within a given sphere of political ideology, and consequently one that does not embrace all mankind. Mutual respect for sovereign states, regardless of their social, economic and political systems should be the corner stone of our international relations. As Ahmad Shukairy of Saudi Arabia once propounded at a gathering of the Political Committee of the General Assembly of the United Nations, "what is peaceful co-existence if we cannot accept the doctrines of others, the ideologies of others, the social orders of others, and the economic systems of others."

There are many internal complications that could arise from affiliation with organizations that exist on a bloc basis. These organizations usually compete for affiliation among the developing countries and use the opportunity to introduce cold war tactics and intrigue into the areas. This is seen particularly in the Trade Union movements. Affiliation for example with the ICFTU could bind us with certain actions which may not be in the best economic interest of the Caribbean area. Certain requests and directives from the headquarters which will certainly be outside the Caribbean and thus would not have the interest of the area foremost would have to be followed. Further, affiliation with the ICFTU means non-recognitions of the WFTU and this runs contrary to the theory and practice of peaceful co-existence as dealt with above. So we have two large sectional organizations each claiming to represent the interest of labor, one of communist orientation and the other (a paradox in itself) or capitalist orientation. Now since capitalism was and still is one of the major diseases arresting the economic growth of the Caribbean, then we should not align ourselves with the ICFTU, for this would serve only to guarantee our continued exploitation at the whims and fancies of wealthy western capitalists and industrialists. On the other hand, since the history of labor in the Caribbean with its plantation system has more in common with feudal Czarist Russia, then we may benefit from the experiences of the 1917 revolution. These benefits, however, can be obtained without affiliation to the WFTU which will only introduce cold war power politics into the area from the other side of the Atlantic. Therefore, if we are to remain outside these intrigues which serve us no useful purpose except where they could be exploited, there should be no affiliation either way. The Caribbean Labor Congress as an entity in itself, and not in its present condition, should be sufficient.

In addition to the above, the Christian religious institutions that we have unfortunately inherited from colonial days is rapidly being exploited not only by homosexuals but by American evangelist extremists and self-appointed missionaries who turn the minds of suffering people from seeking redress and participating in more meaningful activities. The Christian Anti-Communist Crusade under Schwarts and Crane has already made serious inroads in the area with its Christian dogma and cold war intrigue. Guyana has quite a task in removing them. Prayers will not solve our problems for they never do solve problems. We have to bend our backs and broaden our minds if we want any form of progress.

Political and military alliances seldom exist without economic entanglements. There is the lamented case of Puerto Rico, a vassal of the U.S.A. which feigns independence. This country is so economically bound to the imperial power that all that is now necessary is to proclaim it another state. And here we are, asking Canada to take over the defense of the smaller islands. Can't we learn from experience? Do we not hear of the inhuman treatment of Puerto Ricans in the USA? Do we not know the appalling conditions under which Eskimos and Indians exist in Canada?

The Caribbean must be politically free to search for markets for its products in every corner of the globe and not only with Canada as some Canadian businessmen and West Indians who should know better would have it. Our economic viability thus depends on our political freedom and sovereignty so that we can search for these markets without bowing to the threats of any power. We must not therefore depend on any one bloc or country for economic assistance and whenever this assistance becomes necessary it should be obtained outside the confines of political ideologies for, as Jose Marti said, "The country that buys commands. The country that sells obeys. Trade must be balanced to ensure freedom. A country that wants to die sells to only one country, a country that wants to survive sells to more than one. Excessive influence of our country on the trade of another turns into political influence."

Membership in regional organizations like the OAS can be beneficial but certainly not under the existing conditions, for our sovereignty can very easily be undermined. Let us recall the abortive Bay of Pigs invasion of the sovereign state of Cuba in 1961 and we will remember which country backed that invasion and violated the charter of the OAS. Let us also recall the most recent American invasion of the Dominican Republic, also a sovereign state, again in violation of the charter. Is this therefore an organization that we want membership in? It should now be very obvious to us that the champion of the so-called "free world" also holds the record for violating charters while masquerading behind its membership in organizations. Again the expulsion of Cuba from the OAS in 1962 under American pressure makes a mockery of peaceful coexistence. The Alliance for Progress has failed miserably for it was never designed to promote genuine progress. Let us keep out of the OAS.

As we look around us today, we see a world hopelessly and irreconcilably torn into two opposing ideological camps and we should strive to avoid being committed in any way to either one. In so doing, we will avoid any obligation or action which may be to the detriment of our economic growth and political freedom. Alignment with either one of these blocs has the tendency of drawing us into conflicts when we least desire such. We are not in the arms race and should never aim to be for we will only be hastening our own destruction. We can dwell together in unity without them. We have instead to be on the alert to forestall any attempt at installing bases in the area or we shall be classified as "killing grounds" and therefore destined to play a role along with Canada in serving as decoys for Washington and New York. I say this because one Caribbean Territory, no sooner had it achieved its independence than it publicly announced its willingness to have U.S. bases on its soil.

The independent policy that a United Caribbean should follow must be based on the principles set out in the United Nations Charter and at the Bandung and Belgrave Conferences of non-aligned countries, for only thus can imperialism and neo-colonialism be eradicated from the Caribbean.

**Kerwyn Morris is a retired civil servant and, for many years, was Chief Fisheries Officer of St. Vincent. He presently lives in St Vincent and the Grenadines.**

## 9   HISTORICAL MATERIALISM AND CARIBBEAN DESTINY

By Kerwyn L. Morris

(Taken from Flambeau, Number 7, March 1967)

The world today presents a scene of bitter clashes and fierce contradictions. Governments rise and fall, "democratic countries" deny what they preach and the victims of the ghastly betrayal are rightly taking to arms. As the stalwart Afro-American writer WE.B. DuBois said, "the problem of the twentieth century is the problem of the color line." The U.S.A., Britain, South Africa and Zimbabwe (Rhodesia) are proving him right as the political and economic relationships between the developed and "underdeveloped" countries of the world unfold day by day as the politics and economics of color.

In the Caribbean, clashes and conflicts also exist, and the effete and senile reactionaries (the defenders of the status quo) and the youth (the advocates of change) are locked in deadly combat. Serious upheavals are near at hand and violence is fast becoming the only path left open for the people, the true and real makers of history to effect their long overdue liberation from colonial and imperial bondage. By historical necessity and the necessity of human freedom and dignity, the back of colonialism will soon be dealt its final blow. The following decades will consequently be filled with resounding victories and overwhelming joy for some (the suffering and toiling masses), and with unending upsets and disappointments for others (those who direct their energies contrary to the dictates of historical necessity and attempt to turn back the hands of time). Their defeat is as certain as tomorrow's sunrise. For the youth and the masses there lies ahead a long period of intense struggle and tireless efforts if anything like unity and solidarity are to be achieved in the Caribbean.

There are several concepts of history and its making which should be examined if the people are to recognize and play their respective roles in shaping and developing their society, or better still in determining the destiny of the Caribbean.

In view of the fact that Christianity is rampant in the area and that its influence is significant in some way, it is important that its philosophy of history be looked into however lightly. This philosophy that Christianity preaches is outlined by St. Augustine in his work *de civitate dei* (the City of God). Augustine was a North African from

Carthage (now around Libya) of mixed Negro-Berber descent who flourished in the fifth century A.D. In the U.S.A. today he would be called a negro by the white power structure and its sociologists. He claimed that history follows a linear progression from the fall of Lucifer the original bearer of light to the imaginary kingdom of heaven, and that this progression proceeds independent of man. That man, therefore, is only a toy in the progression directed by the extraneous force. The road from this secular state to the long promised but never yet seen ecclesiastical one can be followed by man only through Christian obedience and tolerance. Self-expression and exertion are therefore incompatible with the process of Christian history which is not concerned with the social, political and economic degradation of our society, but with some distant reward. It is only the enemies of human development that can teach us not to expect any improvement in the secular state. It is only the enemies of social development that will instruct us not to prepare for any social transition and maliciously direct our meaningful energies elsewhere.

The defenders of the faith may argue that it assists in educational programs in Africa, Asia, Latin America and the Caribbean, but what they fail to note is the time and energy wasted on efforts of conversion. Why must conversion accompany education? Do non-believers not have the ability to absorb what is being taught? There seems to me to be no relationship between being a Christian and education except where favoritism and patronization are concerned. In Kenya some years ago it was no surprise when Jomo "Mzee" Kenyatta opened his independent schools, because the Presbyterian Missionary schools refused to teach Kikuyu females who had been circumcised according to their customs. Clearly where Christianity is concerned with education other motives are involved. The blind can see this.

Let us now turn to the more rational schools of thought and see what their concepts of history are like. These are the schools that claim man makes his own history without the aid of any extra-terrestrial force. One of these schools holds that individuals are the ones who make history and the other that the masses of people are the true makers of history. The imperialist powers subscribe to the former school while the socialist states and most underdeveloped countries adhere to the latter. Upon examination of the history of colonialism and imperialism, we find the names of individuals most outstanding as makers of history! We also find that these men were in some way responsible for the untold loss of lives of the people who were courageous enough to resist their imperial designs. The cult of individualism – the glorification of military stardom, is thus the core of the imperialist concept of history, and it is this ravenous egoism that did so much to foster the ideas of private property and capitalism.

The other school holds that the masses of people are the true makers of history as all colonial peoples are finding out today. If Cetshwayo, Osei Tutu, Queen Zhinga of Matamba, and Usuman dan Fodio did not have the support of the masses of people they never would have accomplished what they did. The masses of people are the ones who will mold their destiny according to historical necessity and the necessity to be free. It is they who will prepare the conditions for the transition of the new social system. It is they who will call the tunes of the revolution, and it is they who will bind themselves into movements of national liberation for they still do not enjoy the fruits of their labor.

To understand the role of the masses of the people and individuals who may lead them in making history, we must first grasp the concept of historical materialism, the science of general laws of the development of society. Hegel developed the principle and formulated what is now known as the Hegelian triad (thesis, antithesis and synthesis), but it was Karl Marx who applied these ideas to the materialist theory of social development. The dialectics therefore now became a sort of guide or method of approach to social development. Let us for example take our present status quo as the thesis and we will find that within the society exists the anti-thesis or contradictions or negations, or opposites, whichever we may choose to call them. In other words, existing in our society are conditions that necessitate changing as time, history and social development move on, but are not changed. The thesis (status quo) and antithesis (contradiction) therefore enter into continuous reaction with each other in various ways until a synthesis or outcome of the clashes is arrived at. This idea of negations is extremely important in analyzing social development for it tells us at what stage of development a society is at a given time. In all societies, ours being no exception, development proceeds in such a way that the contradictions are forced to reveal themselves. With this revelation a struggle follows, which inevitably ends in the destruction of the old forms and the emergence of new ones – the synthesis. Social development thus necessitates a struggle and the type of struggle indicates the level of development. Hairoun (St. Vincent) is in the midst of a struggle and it is not hard to see the type of struggle taking place. The guardians of the thesis (status quo) who relish in its corruption are face to face with the might of the antithesis, and a vendetta to the death is on.

Historical materialism then, when used as a method for analyzing our particular situation tells us why the police harass students abroad and hunt down progressive elements within the society. It tells us why suitably qualified native personnel are placed second to foreigners – because the foreign personnel itself contains an element of corruption and will try to preserve the status quo. It tell us why old Savio Lee took such a reactionary stand and why such heavy blows were rained down on him. But above all, it tells us that the role of the protectors of the thesis will soon be ended for historical necessity knows no compromise and the necessity of human freedom, dignity and development no alternative. Historical materialism tells us why social revolutions occur and why they are significant in the historical process. It is the methodological basis of all other social sciences for it allows true historians, economists and politicians to understand the intricate network of social phenomena and to determine the place and significance of each phenomenon in social life. It allows us also to understand the roles of people and individuals in social development.] Historical necessity is that which naturally follows from the internal conditions and social phenomena, and is therefore bound to take place. If the internal conditions in Hairoun necessitate a revolution then by necessity this revolution will occur. Social revolutions always take place by necessity. Of course the Christian philosophy of history does not recognize historical necessity in this sense for it claims, as I have said, that the entire historical process is determined by an outside force and that man is but a chess man in the hands of providence. *How mistaken they are.*

Freedom is the result of historical and social development and is an indispensable prerequisite for the growth of any society, ours being no exception. Today we are at the point of being "granted" a so-called advanced constitution, but the liberation of colonial territories is not a grant to the exploited. It is historical necessity at work for the liberation of colonial peoples is something that is inevitable. It is something that these people are calling for sometimes with arms and it is only in avoidance of a showdown that liberation is "granted" to subjugated peoples. Colonialism and imperialism have forced us, their victims, to conspire and rebel against them and the synthesis of this struggle is inevitable for nothing stops historical necessity. Victories, it must be remembered, are not always foreseen for they are not always determined by the size of armies, the quality and quantity of weapons or the presence of warships. Strategic and psychological calculations in the light of historical necessity also bring resounding victories. Guerilla warfare has brought many a victory over conventional warfare and as long as the necessity for freedom exists (and it always will), then it will be pursued to a victorious end no matter what method may be chosen.

Having seen that people and not any other force make history, we now ask ourselves of what importance are these people and their leaders in the historical process, and what is the relationship between them. By the people or masses I do not intend to convey them as the "rabble" or "common crowd" as the bourgeoisie describe them; I mean the people whose tireless labor has been exploited for centuries. If we agree that material production is the basis of social life and that the working people constitute the chief productive force, then we must also agree that these same people are the decisive force in social development. The more active these people are and the more diversified in material production, the more pressing is the need for experienced and mature leaders; leaders aware of the inevitability of historical necessity and familiar with historical materialism; leaders who have clearly seen the objective and subjective laws of the society in operation; leaders who can reflect the aspirations of the people at all times, for if they fail to do so, they shall be wiped from the scene of history never to return. The role of leaders is very significant in any movement, for leaders or great men do not appear by chance but by historical necessity – when the conditions are ripe. Such men come to the fore generally in a period of radical revolutionary change in the society. They emerge because they understand the objective course of the historical process, recognize the needs of a developing society, and know how to satisfy the requirements in order to improve human life. As Ibn Khaldun of Tunis said (1370 A.D.) the leader must "accommodate the sentiments and desires of the people and share his power with them," for no man is greater than the people he leads. He must possess qualities that allow him to serve the social needs of his time and he must never forget that his strength lies in his contact with the people whom historical necessity has brought him to lead and in his ability to organize them.

The people may be organized into what is called a national liberation movement, for the purpose of securing the total liberation of the nation or island as it may be, from the forces that arrest its development – colonialism, imperialism, and neo-colonialism. These movements should be formed in all the islands and should have close links with each other.

The development of the national liberation struggle entered a new phase as a result of the Second World War. Many colonies, it will be recalled, were drawn into the maelstrom of war and some of them in Africa and Asia actually became the scene of human butcher stalls. The requirements of the war economy compelled the colonial and imperial powers to accelerate the development of certain industries in their colonial possessions and this led to a rapid development of the indigenous proletariat. In 1939, more than two-thirds of humanity was under the colonial yoke but between 1945 and 1960 more than 1,500 million people liberated themselves and took the part of independent development. Today there remains only 1.5% of the world's population under colonialism. 97% of the Asian land mass contains sovereign states while 75% of Africa is liberated. Of the one hundred odd countries represented at the United Nations, one-half of them are in Asia and Africa. Where is the Caribbean? Jamaica, Trinidad and Tobago, Guyana and Barbados have gone their separate ways. Why are the remaining people of the Caribbean still under colonialism, is it that we love it? Why are there no liberation movements in the area and why have all the significant changes that have taken place in the colonial world bypassed the Caribbean?

The inevitable collapse of the colonial system in Africa and Asia is the result of a most powerful upsurge of national liberation movements and social and political consciousness among the people – the manifestations of historical necessity and the necessity of human freedom and dignity. And with the break up of the system and its final disappearance in Africa, Asia, Latin America, and the Caribbean, some of the most shameful and horrid pages in the annals of imperialist history will have been turned over. The defenders of the system are helplessly watching its last barricades fall day by day while they scramble for the last favors. They try in every fraudulent way to belittle the role and significance of liberation movements or anything resembling them and maliciously spread the myth that colonial independence is not won as a result of the struggle of the colonial peoples but rather is "granted" or more stylishly "guided" to it by their masters. How then upon the achievement of independence the colonies are still found (after "guidance") to be underdeveloped? We should by now understand that the only .guidance we ever knew was along the path of perpetual underdevelopment. The imperial powers themselves maintain the view that no people of any colony is ever ready enough for independence, that is until the people rise up against their alien rule (Algeria, U.A.R., Sudan, India, Kenya [Mau Mau], Ghana, Viet Nam) and expel them. Why have we not yet shaken off our rule by foreign powers? Colonial powers leave only when the action of the people they rule demand that they take their exit. They never depart voluntarily so let our actions show that we want the Caribbean to be ruled by Caribbeans.

The basis for liberation has always been a struggle by the people and we cannot expect our liberation until our people rise up and demand it themselves. The people of each island must themselves choose the means of effecting their liberation and they should be concerned with winning their liberation with the minimum of human losses. We must first therefore try to remove the colonial powers by peaceful means, but if this fails, then there is no alternative but the use of arms. In the period 1945-1955, more than ten countries were forced to take up arms in order to expel the colonialists, while from 1956 to 1962 thirty-three out of thirty-five colonies won their liberation without recourse to arms. How shall ours be won?

The efforts of national liberation movements are by no means confined to the elimination of oppression and subservience but are broadened to create the material basis for economic development after the achievement of political independence. The obtaining of this independence is only the first phase of the revolution for national liberation, for complete national liberation means also economic independence. The job of building the nation's economy now comes to the forefront of the struggle. There are some people who hold the view that economic independence must precede political independence, but I think it is the other way around. How can we ever have any economic independence if we do not have the political authority to direct *all* the phases of our economic planning?

There are many countries that have won political independence but still today remain appendages of world capitalist economy and division of industrial labor. The road of economic development must be chosen by the liberated people themselves for they must decide their own destiny. The inherited colonial economic system is incapable of leading us toward economic independence for it was never designed to do this as the economic conditions of all present and former colonies reveal. The development of the state sector is decisive in any country. If the state owns the main branches of the country's economy, then it places itself in a position to direct and control the economy, and at the same time combat the dominance of foreign monopolies and break up the colonial economic structure. It is no mistake that the majority of countries liberated from colonialism have chosen the triumphant path of building socialism. At the third Afro-Asian Solidarity Conference held in Tanganyika, February 1963, the countries attending proposed the nationalization of the investments of the imperialist monopolies. This also was no mistake.

Various forms of social and economic changes are currently being introduced in the developing countries to bridge the gap in the standards of living and to raise the level of their economies. What changes are we attempting in the Caribbean? What changes can we make when no one wants to deviate from the colonial norm? Everyone is afraid of being branded and having to live on the fringes of the colonial society. But the patience of the people of the Caribbean is fast running out and soon a new phase will (confrontation of the thesis and antithesis) occur by historical necessity. It is then that the might of the reactionaries will be tested. It is then that the masses, the true makers of history will take over the machinery of government and direct their own development.

We need a society without poverty and exploitation, without social injustice, and without any form of oppression. We need a society without corruption in which all concerned would be united in true brotherhood rather than divided into antagonistic socio-economic classes. We need a society founded on socialism that would provide the wellbeing of all, a society that will provide equality, collectivism, liberty and creative labor, a society that would foster the free development of each for this is the basis for the free development of all. Socialism equates with the vital interests of all the working people – the people whose role in the society is significant, and this is exactly what we need in the Caribbean for any meaningful progress to take place. If we follow this path, the path that most liberated areas are following today, then we can't possibly be misled.

**Kerwyn Morris is a retired civil servant and, for many years, was Chief Fisheries Officer of St. Vincent. He presently lives in St Vincent and the Grenadines.**

## 10    SOCIAL AND ECONOMIC PROBLEMS IN THE WINDWARD ISLANDS (1838-65)

### By Woodville Marshall

(Taken from Flambeau, Number 8, September 1967)

    What most of these Negro laborers wanted (after emancipation) was the unfettered opportunity to cultivate their own lands and to pursue their own interests. Consequently, the "irksome" character of labor-rent and conditional tenancy acted as spurs to their defection from estate labor and aggravated the condition of labor relations. In a free society the majority of laborers could be kept easily and contentedly on the estates only by the operation of the incentives of kind treatment, secure tenancy, fair wages and the freedom to dispose of their labor. The obvious reform, therefore, was the separation of labor from rent and the institution of moderate money rent and unconditional labor contracts. Such a reform was more likely than any other system both to create a reservoir of potential labor in an estate tenantry and to stabilize the labor market by "doing away", as Stipendiary Magistrate Roach said, "with ceaseless complaints and bickerings" and by allowing labor to seek the best market and employers to recruit and retain only what labor they required. But these suggestions were entertained only in a few cases; "the old leaven of slavery," as Bennett said, still worked "in the planters' brain" to prevent any such modification of traditional patterns.

    The laborers reacted to this coercive policy by withdrawing in large numbers from regular estate labor and sometimes from estate labor altogether. Since the planters' policy was obviously designed to limit rather than consolidate the Negroes' freedom, it devolved on the Negroes to seek to establish the primacy of their own interests. The fluctuation and decline in the amount of labor given to the estates were, therefore, a reflection of the Negroes' efforts and the limited success in attaining this objective. The determination was expressed in a variety of ways. Firstly, many women and children left estate labor. The women remained at home to make their husbands' houses "comfortable" and to tend their provision grounds. Secondly, despite the opposition of the planters, a substantial portion of the labor force either emigrated permanently to Trinidad or participated in the seasonal migrations during the crop to exploit the high wages which were being paid in that island; and this "systematic emigration," as Hincks described it in 1861, continued throughout the period. Thirdly, an increasing number of laborers sought employment away from the sugar estates. There was a significant increase in the number of persons employed in the various trades, in shop keeping, fishing, charcoal manufacture, firewood and logwood cutting, and in cocoa and arrowroot production. Fourthly, and most important, a substantial minority of the laborers succeeded in establishing an existence almost completely independent of the estates on the basis of possession of fairly extensive portions of leasehold and freehold land. This was the emergence of the peasantry which represented the Negroes' fullest exploitation of the opportunities offered by their emancipation.

This combination of factors produced a sharp decline both in the amount of labor given to the estates and in the numerical strength of the traditional labor force. The independent or semi-independent status of the smallholders and peasants rendered regular estate labor a secondary consideration, a supplementary support of their new freedom. They worked on the estates in their "spare time" and not only when the estates required their services. The residents, for their part, sought every means to escape their contractual obligations; they tried to secure the financial advantages of non-resident labor without technically becoming non-resident; they gave priority in cultivation to their own gardens. The nine hour day was progressively reduced to seven and occasionally to six hours by the laborers and irregularity in attendance deprived the estates of at least a third of the labor of their gangs. This "inconvenience" to the planters was greatly increased by the simultaneous numerical decline of the labor force. At a conservative estimate, the estates lost completely about a third of their labor force in the first decade of the period, and only fairly substantial immigration prevented this proportion from rising to about a half by the end of the period as a result of the continuous emigration and the expansion of the peasant and smallholding classes.

The planters' reaction to these serious problems revealed once again the pernicious character and effect of their habituation. This habituation had been created mainly by the character of the social and economic organization of the recent past, but at the same time an additional degree of irresponsibility had been induced by the existence of general absentee ownership and the colonial-commercial connection to Britain. Both of these effectively inhibited self-criticism among the planters and provided a pretext for their inaction; the planters could assert shrilly and perpetually that factors operating outside of the islands or outside their own control were mainly if not solely responsible for the decline in the sugar industry. They refused to recognize even a partial responsibility for the existing situation, and they failed to realize that they could significantly improve this situation and their own fortunes by their own efforts and initiative. Rather, they saw the causes of the industry's misfortunes in British humanitarian and commercial policy and in the natural "apathy and indolence" of their Negro labor force. Therefore, they sat on their ailing el dorados waiting for a British parliamentary dispensation, the magic wand that would instantly recall the prosperity of the early eighteenth century. As Miss Cumpston has written, "it was a long habituated outlook, a stabilized reaction for them to lean on outside aid, even to hold out the begging bowl."

For this reason their own recommendations for the restoration of the stability of the industry were sterile contributions to the discussion since, if implemented, they could only perpetuate an old and sickly condition, not improve it. Continued protection for British West Indian sugar, frequent financial aid from Britain, and in particular British assisted and sponsored immigration could provide little more than a respite in the absence of any evidence of the planters' intention to help themselves by instituting the necessary reforms in the structure and organization of the industry. Yet these were the sum total of their recommendations, and the limit of their unforced awareness of their enveloping problems.

Fortunately the hard realities of the situation both at home and in Britain ensured that the planters' recommendations would never be fully accepted and that consequently other avenues of development would at least be explored. The Free Traders finally carried the day despite the efforts of Lord George Bentinck and the gallant "last stand of the West Indian interest" though there was the small consolation prize for the planters of postponement of full equalization of the sugar duties until 1854. Financial aid never amounted to much; the islands were too small and insignificant to merit great attention from the Colonial Office and private capital had found more profitable fields of investment in railway construction, etc. But a few crumbs of comfort were offered by the British Government in the form of parliamentary loans during and after the crisis of 1846-48. Finally, and most important for the planters, the islands could not afford and therefore never received that substantial immigration which would have created the conditions of dependent labor which the planters required and which alone would have justified the massive expenditure. Nor could the planters make a sound case of immigrant labor; wages remained low, the tenancy regulations remained harsh, and partly in consequence there was continuous emigration. Immigration into the Windwards was therefore, "like putting water into a sieve," as a Colonial Office memo declared in 1835. Most of the 11,000 immigrants which arrived during the period never conferred any lasting benefit on the sugar industry; some emigrated and many of the others escaped the estates for smallholding activity as soon as their contracts expired.

The general failure forced the planters to find other solutions for the problems of capital and labor. For most of the period they ignored all the major reforms that were suggested and they only managed to introduce – and then only as a short term expedient – one innovation of impressive potential. The attempt to relieve the estates of their indebtedness and encumbrance was not made until the "fifties and sixties" through the operation of the Encumbered Estates Act; and it was only the extended use of metayage cultivation in all the islands except St. Vincent which provided a partial solution for the problem of capital shortage and labor supply during and after the crisis of 1846-48. But this innovation was robbed of a great part of its relevance by the planters' attitude to it. For them it remained a stop gap (though it achieved permanence in Tobago) rather than an opportunity for basic reorganization of the industry and the society, through the encouragement of the growth of a class of peasant cane farmers and the separation of cultivation from manufacture. Nevertheless, it was mainly due to metayage, and to a lesser extent, to peasant cane-farming and to the few economies in management that were achieved that the sugar industry managed to survive in not too attenuated a form throughout the period.

The main social problem was the problem of the freed Negro: how to bring him fully within the pale of a society which was dominated by rigidly traditionalist and often racist attitudes and values. In short, the problem was that of completing the emancipation of the ex-slaves. The whole society had been "reconstructed," the fact of emancipation demanded speedy and fundamental adjustment of the planters' attitudes and policies to ensure the transformation of their oligarchic industrial empires into broader based dynamic societies. The necessity for this transformation was made even more urgent as the period developed by the continuing decline of the sugar industry and more important, by the emergence of a large class of smallholders and peasants, which testified to the general industriousness of the Negroes and to the constructive role they were playing in the community. What was needed, in particular, was the provision both of opportunity for the full participation of the new citizens in all aspects of the community's life, and of those vital social services which would equip the army of new citizens for its new role in society and which, in any case, were its right and due.

This problem, as in economic development, resolved itself into a clash between two diametrically opposed objectives. The majority of the

Negroes made it clear from the beginning that they would behave like freemen, not like dependents on the estates; they would consult their own interests first and they would be vigilant to see that their new rights would not be too seriously infringed upon, even if they could not demand that these rights should be allowed their fullest exercise. Whenever a direct threat to these rights seemed to materialize they wrote petitions and memorials, or they resorted to strike action, or they rioted. In all these actions there was the expression both of a determination to maintain their new status and of a claim for greater consideration and a degree of responsible participation in the society. And most important of all, the industry and initiative of many of them led to the emergence of a peasantry, which itself offered a dynamic and alternative basis for the development of the society.

These attitudes and objectives naturally clashed with those of the planters. For the latter, emancipation was not a major social revolution; it was a labor problem with an implied and ominous threat to their own social and economic preeminence. The maintenance of this position was for them the "true interests" of the society and consequently every effort was made to perpetuate the policies and the social structure of a past age since these seemed the best guarantee of the existence of the traditional structure. Therefore, the planters used all the considerable influence and power at their command to ensure that their own positions would not be challenged and that the Negroes should remain almost as subordinate to their former masters as when they were slaves and apprentices.

The planters' power was the irresistible factor in the situation. This power which was founded on their ownership and control of the major sector of the economy and maintained by an extremely narrow elective franchise and by participation in some of the judicial functions was unscrupulously deployed to ensure that, in this case, their own objectives would in large measure be achieved. Consequently, a small class of planters and planters' nominees wielded unchallenged political power throughout the period, and as far as their abilities would allow them administered the governmental machine in their own interests. They successfully resisted most of the attempts to loosen their grip, and this success in perpetuating their own selfish and inefficient rule was largely responsible for the backwardness in political, constitutional and social development which has characterized the existence of the Windward Islands. The planters seemed determined not to involve the whole of the population, or at least a larger section of it, in any of the functions of society except those of estate labor. Though they failed to prevent the emergence of a peasantry they succeeded in denying it effective political expression.

In the immediate context, neither of the main prerequisites for healthy social development was heeded. Firstly, the vast majority of the Negroes were denied all regular means of political expression while the planter class was confirmed in its oligarchic control. The elective franchise was deliberately kept limited and exclusive by means of high property qualifications and professional status. This was doubly unfortunate. Since most of the franchises made a mockery of the representative principle and practice and since the Assemblies were sadly deficient in able personnel, it would have been both wise and politic if the planters had attempted to repair their deficiencies by involving more of the Negroes and, particularly the peasantry, in the political life of the islands. The perpetuation of this condition of exclusion helped therefore to ensure the final condemnation and extinction of the Representative System, and it also produced a dangerous degree of frustration among some of the Negroes.

Secondly, little attention was paid to the establishment or extension of the social services, those "objects of great importance" as Sir Charles Edward Grey called them, which were vital to the construction of a new society after a period of slavery. Little revenue was available for this purpose, but what little there was could have been more beneficially applied to the needs of the whole community. But the planters possessed a set of priorities in social and economic policy which had little relation to the objective situation. Fairly substantial sums of private and public capital were expended on a wide variety of immigration schemes, but only paltry sums were irregularly voted and applied to vital services like the establishment of a Poor Relief system and the extension or nationalization of the medical and health services. In particular, the provision of a system of popular education which should have been top priority in a country "but lately emerged from the darkness of slavery into the full light of freedom," received scant attention despite the initial aid provided by the British government and the Mico Charity. Most planters seemed to regard the education of the Negroes as a "positive evil" since it might "impair their usefulness as laborers."

This general situation naturally deepened the frustration and resentment of the Negro population and increased the chances of a violent explosion. When news of the Morant Bay Riot reached the Windward Islands, it was not surprising therefore, that at least in St. Vincent, the influential members of the community were alarmed while the Negroes clearly exhibited their sympathy for the rioters' cause. Lieutenant Governor Berkeley of St. Vincent reported in 1866:

> There can be little doubt that the sympathies of the lower orders were almost universally enlisted in favor of the malcontents, and it would be hazardous to venture an opinion as to what might have been the effects produced here had a different result befallen the measures adopted for repressing the outbreak in Jamaica.

By this time the crisis signaled the end of a turbulent epoch in West Indian history, it had become clear in the Windward Islands that emancipation was still not complete. The planters still kept and intended to keep the majority of the Negroes in subordinate social, political and economic positions. The possibility of an alternative society based on the full and direct participation and which the rise of the peasantry had rendered a practical proposition, was not recognized; or, if it was recognized, it was ignored. The rejection condemned the Windward Islands to a long period of stagnation in the nineteenth and twentieth centuries.

**Dr Woodville Marshall was Professor of History at the Cave Hill campus of the University of the West Indies in Barbados. He is retired and presently lives in Barbados.**

## 11    EDUCATION AND SOCIAL GOALS

By Kenneth John

(Taken from Flambeau, Number 8, September 1967)

The British Caribbean Area is fast moving from a position of dependence to a new position of formal independence. In 1888 a Commission had referred to the region as a tropical farm of the British Nation, which is what it was. If a new relationship is to be established today in order to invest political independence with some meaning, a lot of work will have to be done in the field of broad education. Problems will have to be defined and goals clarified. For on the one hand there seems to be an affirmation of West Indianization implicit in the quest for independence and its improvised variants, and on the other hand there is a negation of the spirit of West Indian unity evidenced in the fragmentation of the area. Among other things the educational system must be geared to effect some sort of reconciliation between these divergent trends and in so doing to blur the deeper lines of insularity.

Probably the most besetting sin of the region is its lack of a cultural identity. Every group, if it is to have meaningful survival value, must possess a sense of history, have some definite purpose, and must be headed in a direction which it considers desirable. If there is an absence of roots and there are only vague goals the group becomes disoriented and the society so far from being a dynamic entity is cut adrift, as it were. What we need to remedy this defect is a proper history of ourselves highlighting the social origins of our people, not the conventional military and narrowly political history studded with the names of monarchs and battles and dates. There must be a history of ourselves in its own right, no longer must we form a footnote to the history of the imperial power. In this context a proper study of slavery becomes imperative, for it was the crucible whence we sprang an ill-formed society.

As ex-slaves we should be taught that our history did not begin on the docks in the Caribbean or at the slave markets on the African coast. Most of us came from Africa and many of us are of Asian extraction. A proper study of Africa may lead us to discover, for instance, that although the standard of civilization was not uniformly high throughout the continent, it certainly did not present the picture of utter barbarity which is commonly taught to us. We need to know, too, that there is nothing inherently shameful about our slave past. It would save a lot of embarrassment if we knew that slavery was a universal institution, though it assumed a particular form in the West Indies. And we should play up the role of the freedom fighters among the slaves who instituted any number of slave revolts and demonstrated many other forms of resistance. In other words, though history should aim at a measure of objectivity, the interpretation of the neutral facts should be influenced by the needs of the present.

But education in the West Indies is not well integrated with the social system. It has always been a pale imitation of the British educational system. The original impulse to West Indian Education came to meet a social need as defined by the colonial power. After Emancipation came the so-called Negro Question. It dawned suddenly on the British that slavery was not the best training ground for a people it was about to let loose in a new free society. It was felt that the negro who was alienated and brutalized before abolition would experience untold difficulties in adjusting to the new situation. This problem of incorporation of ex-slaves into the New Society and the lurking fear that the imminent collapse of the social order was a distinct possibility led to the Negro Education Grant which, incidentally, provided more money to be spent on education in the West Indies than was spent in England at the time. But when it is recalled that this education was meant to meet a specific need, the nature of its content could easily be anticipated. The Church was given the official green light to spread the gospel, impose its catechisms and foist its doctrines on the people. Not unnaturally, a heavy emphasis was placed on one's duty to one's neighbor, of the Christian's duty to carry himself lowly and reverently before teachers and pastors, and to be satisfied with that station in life in which it hath pleased God to place him. Tolerance, submissiveness and resignation were the be-all and end-all of immediate post slavery education.

Education drifted on in this undisciplined fashion for a number of years. This has been partly due to the fact that the problem has almost always been defined in the terms of so-called visiting experts rather than by local people who are strategically placed to understand the needs of the society and are prepared to come to grips with the real indigenous difficulties. Eric Williams broke ground only a few years ago when he had an Education Report on Trinidad submitted by an entirely West Indian team of Commissioners. Things are beginning to change, but not nearly fast enough. Until the Cato Report even the University College of the West Indies had been conceived and set up on the basis of reports done by the foreigner. As a direct result West Indian education, including education at the University of the West Indies, has not been generated from within but mainly takes its cue from external promptings, reflecting changes and responding to pressures from outside of the region. This does not speak well for the area, especially as the pivotal role of education in giving vitality and dynamism to a society is beyond question. For a social system to function properly there must be certain built-in qualities which accord it survival value. These include an adaptive element, determinate goals, and mechanisms to provide for the integration of the system. And education is the chief agency through which this resilience can be achieved.

To begin with, the area has to grapple with the problems of rapid population growth which doubles every twenty-five years or so, and the very limited resources which affect levels of living as well as pose a serious political problem. Tourism, which has been regarded as the salvation of the region, also presents some evils. For the society to adapt and properly accommodate the changes which the tourist industry entails, for example, it must legislate for the social control of land use and institute beach control authorities. Some controls should also be placed on the fishing industry to protect local fishermen, and efforts should be made to ensure that the whole pattern of recreational behavior is not adversely affected. Secondly, education in Europe followed in the wake of industrialization and was accordingly streamlined to rationalize an existing state of economic affairs. In the West Indies, on the other hand, education preceded industrialization and produced relatively high rates of literacy which are geared to a pre-industrial society. In fact in many of the West Indian islands the little industrial education has slipped in, so to speak, through the back door by way of a poorly organized apprenticeship system. This is a totally inadequate system to meet the technical needs of the society. In the prevailing scheme of things, as soon as an apprentice feels that he has acquired enough of the skills to permit him an independent existence, he branches off and sets up his own business. What is sorely needed is a bureaucratic system with the establishment of a Standards Board, and the move towards certification. In addition commercial education, which seems to have sprung up in a fit of absentmindedness on the fringes of the general system, should be accorded a place in the curriculum in its own right.

One needs not to go as far as one lecturer in English at the U.W.I. who is supposed to have said that the West Indian can never make a first class English Honors student. Nonetheless, it remains largely true that the finer points of English Literature can never be fully appreciated by the bulk of the West Indians. With this in mind there should be some attempt made to revamp the traditional classical approach to education and deemphasize the role of the literary element in curricula. It is probably symptomatic of the inherited school of thought that attaches great weight to the literary aspect that, instead of being the logical ones to be established first at the U.W.I., the faculties of agriculture and engineering were the last to attract the serious attention of West Indian educationists, or rather, educationists for the West Indies. Just over a century ago DeVerteuil in his history of Trinidad declared that a program of agricultural education was a "must" in the West Indies, but his advice was not heeded for a very long time. In fact there were serious discussions in learned West Indian journals and magazines as to whether or not the negro mind could absorb the teachings of science. Given the values of the society which cast a stigma on all forms of manual labor agricultural students were not forthcoming in sufficient numbers. Many believed that agriculture features too "low" in the syllabus. The teaching profession, as a mobile class in a rigidly stratified society, was obsessed with the notion of status and its external symbols. It was thought unbecoming for teachers to take off their coats and ties, which they had to do to teach agriculture properly. They would not lightly throw away their hard won "respectability." Even when the realities of the situation forced themselves on the population, agricultural education hardly became an integral part of general education. It was taught away from the established centers and institutions, say at the Eastern Caribbean Farm Institute or at Twickenham Park, probably as unfortunate aberrations of the system.

Probably more important than the question of adaptation is the matter of desired goals. The chief goals in the West Indies are a political democracy and racial equality, but unless the educational system is oriented towards making the way possible for the attainment of these goals they will remain unreachable ideals. The people of the region are woefully illiterate and such people find it difficult to understand the world in which they live. It is possible that the illiterate person may possess enough mental equipment to operate effectively at the local level, but he is usually completely overwhelmed by the complexities of the modern international world. One can romanticize about the common sense and basic intelligence of the ordinary man ad nauseum, but unless a certain standard of literacy has been achieved he remains pliant and manipulable to the craft and cunning of the shrewd but literate leader. It means, too, that there will be an immense cleavage in organizations. The officers of any group must attain a certain standard of literacy in order to conduct the business of the body. Where there is a large proportion of illiterate rank-and-file members there can hardly be any sense of internal democracy.

There would be an absence of meaningful dialogue since the illiterates would be suffering severe communication problems, there would be no popular participation in decision-making, and all ideas and rules will flow in a one way traffic from the top. And the way would be left wide open for undetected corruption. It is because of this that the history of most mass organizations in the West Indies – the trade union, the credit union and cooperatives – has been a history of studied corruption. The Friendly Societies have been anything but friendly. They have been the el dorado of many an unscrupulous and rapacious secretary-treasurer. Wells, investigating the workings of West Indian Friendly Societies in the 1940s referred to the widespread organizational exploitation and called for their replacement by National Insurance Schemes.

The other chief aspiration of West Indian society, though some folks seem to think that it is a reality, is racial concord. There is an oral tradition about race in the West Indies that is not reflected in the official literature. There is no greater myth than the racial harmony that is preached and repeated like any church litany, and with about the same spiritual significance attached. Race problems in the West Indies are never confronted, they are shelved or wished away. The origin of the myriad races that make up the inhabitants of the area must be tackled fearlessly and debated openly. One needs to know what it means to be black, colored or white under the present Dispensation. An honest to goodness approach in education must be started. All books – and there are many of them – which, by their underlying anti-black bias subtly inculcate an inferiority complex in the West Indian Negro must be struck off the reading list in schools. Films which hold up African tribal life to ridicule and whose latent purpose is to reinforce the supremacy of white values must not be shown in the West Indies. In our cosmopolitan society, one must be encouraged to probe the roots of cultural differences among the several people as a prelude to tolerance, understanding and mutual respect. In default of this, all sort of distorted philosophies and bizarre cults like Rastafarianism are likely to spring up among the social outcasts who are in desperate search of an ideology which can give them an identity, respect, and some meaningful existence in the prevailing scheme of things.

Integration of the society will come about as a result of the efforts made to realize the goals of a political democracy and racial equality. For if these efforts are sincerely made the elitist concept of democracy now in vogue, as well as the existing rigidly stratified social structure that is galvanized by the race and color theme, will both go by the board. But so long as our educational system is not tailored to meet the demands of the society and there is no linkage between education and experience, so long will our society remain sick to the point of schizophrenia, symptoms of which it is increasingly putting on display.

**Dr Kenneth John holds a Ph.D. in Political Science from Manchester University. He is a newspaper columnist and a practicing lawyer in St Vincent and the Grenadines**

## 12 SOME POLITICAL ASPECTS OF INDEPENDENCE

By E. Augustus & W. Rodney

(Taken from Flambeau, Number 8, September 1967)

Without indulging in any invective, it can be stated that colonialism meant for all territories of the West Indies a subjection to metropolitan interests. If political independence is not to be purely nominal, it is imperative that we seize the opportunity now afforded us for the first time to reorganize our society in our own interests.

A sound knowledge and understanding of the pure colonial model as well as of our more recent transitional history is essential to our future orientation. In the political sphere there are three legacies of colonialism which merit attention. Firstly, there is the piecemeal approach to problems, which must give way to total planning. Secondly, there is the unfortunate habit of looking outside for the solutions of internal problems – the running home to London to save the Federation; the futile hopes that Britain in her benevolence would maintain the same system of preferences in favor of the West Indies once she gains her independence of these islands. Thirdly, there is the authoritarian tradition bequeathed by the system of imperial relationships. Two important organs will suffice to pinpoint this: the political parties and the trade unions. Democracy can only work when the people are given clear alternatives and when the machinery is present so that the masses participate in the decision-making processes. This does not really apply to our political parties. In the West Indies there has been plenty of "political trickstering" but little sincere attempt to expose the population to arguments which may enable them to make rational and informed decisions. Nearly all the islands have trade unions which reduce democracy to a farce, many decisions being taken even without the consultation of the members. Wherever the semblance of popular support for the middle and upper sections of our community is achieved it is primarily because they possess a monopoly of the propaganda machinery and/or because the lower sections have no real choice. It is incumbent on any government to redress this imbalance.

The colonial attitudes must go, to be replaced by a systematic ideology. All that ideology implies is the complex of values, ends and means which have been decided on in the light of our own objective situation. It may well be that we can adopt some fundamental way of looking at the world from other communities and that we can borrow various techniques used by countries in a similar position; but to say that one is a British Labor Party Socialist, or even a Marxist-Leninist, is quite meaningless. Any ideology we embrace must be flexible enough to admit of synthesis, but definitive enough to exclude "revisionism" in the pejorative sense. Certain social and economic ends have already been posited and may be summarized as follows:

1. Social
   a. the integration of the community
   b. the maximization of individual dignity

2. Economic
   a. the full exploitation of the potential wealth of the community
   b. a more equitable distribution of such wealth

The perennial political problem of who is to govern must be given adequate attention. Actual power in a society such as ours tends to be in the hands of elites. Since 1938 a Middle class elite group has ruled in most of the islands. The members of this group are experts at making and breaking constitutions, but insofar as values are concerned they have little to offer the community, and their departure would be welcome even if they all have to be pensioned off. The only replacement for the present "establishment" are those who can be counted on to define clear goals in a more objective manner. That is to say, while this new elite may be middle class it will not share middle class biases. One has only to consider by way of example that the middle class intelligentsia is more susceptible to revolutionary ideas than the proletariat to realize that the idea of such leadership is by no means strange. The emphasis is laid on group leadership rather than on the elevation of a single individual since although the charisma of a particular leader is useful and virtually inevitable in a small community, it is unwise to perpetuate the personal cultism which now exists in West Indian politics. It is not overoptimistic to suppose that the U.W.I can produce such an elite group. In fact, this is one of the few ways in which it can justify its existence. The urbane detachment of the British University is a luxury that we cannot afford with our limited resources, the dynamic role of the Latin American Universities being far more relevant.

It is our contention that the desired reforms cannot be brought about by gradualism, and since they will not come about by spontaneous generation they have to be pushed through in a manner that is bound to invite opposition. As it is, the present elites show no sign of willingness to abdicate power and, indeed, the likelihood is that attempts will be made to freeze the political situation in a way that would exclude interlopers. However, granted that the new elite achieves power through the normal channels, when they attempt to implement social and economic policies which are relatively more beneficial to lower sections, certain groups will engage in increased activity designed to prevent this. The primacy of politics lies in the fact that it not only supervenes the clashing of interests, but prescribes which interests may present themselves at the contest. The counter-elite group would be powerful and highly articulate, and government must take vigorous measures if it is to compete successfully against them. One way to eliminate them as serious competitors for popular support is to break their monopoly control of propaganda agencies. It is impossible to implement social reform when the largest circulating daily belongs to a reactionary opposition. The implications here would appear to be a destruction of certain essential civil liberties and the opposition would inevitably appear under guise of champions of democratic freedoms such as freedom of the press. A little reflection shows that freedom of the press in the West Indies has merely meant the monopoly control of the most important agency for the dissemination of information by those in a financially superior position. It must be conceded that any attempt to implement sweeping reorganization will demand an increase in the authoritarian element of government, but it shall be argued further that this need not necessarily conflict with popular participation and its justification is that in any case it is a transitional phenomenon.

  The most important task of government would be to mobilize the ordinary people and make them a functioning part of the decision making machinery. The elite must proceed on the assumption that the vast majority of the people are capable of envisaging "the good society" but in practice seldom achieve clarity for a number of reasons. Firstly, they lack the necessary information about alternatives and their implications. Secondly, owing to the fact that their experience is often limited by the geographical and social area in which they exist, as well as by lack of educational opportunities, they are denied certain essential comparative tools of analysis. Thirdly, more often than not they think in terms of self rather than community and hence cannot arrive at a total picture. Complete mobilization in the pursuit of common goals is no easy task and some of the pitfalls in the paths of the attempt should be pointed out. Firstly, there is the possibility that full mobilization will not take place. Traditionalism especially in the rural areas may stand as a barrier to progress, and while it is relatively easy to justify high handed treatment of counter-elites, it is another matter to coerce sections of the populace into doing what is supposedly for their own good. This introduces us to the second trap, and that is the tendency for the ruling elite to confuse what it feels to be in the best interests of the people with what the people themselves feel are in their own best interests. Finally, mobilization can take the form of propagandizing in the vicious sense, where high pressure techniques are used to fog the minds of people so that what comes out of them is really what was intended should come out. If a government can achieve such a feat it would have justified its claim to govern, but we place this outside of present realities. Optimism for success of political mobilization is based on the fact that if sociological and economic insights are reasonably accurate, then one can say that the program will accord with the fundamental aspirations of the people, and they themselves will articulate them when given the opportunity.

To make the people the audience of mass media of communication is essential but not enough. It is clear that a problem of communication exists on the psychological level. Education is the only answer to this and must be the new dynamic in the state. If this has not been already appreciated, then we state explicitly that the education system must be redesigned both in form and spirit to suit the new ends of the nation.

Earlier the possibility of opposition and its treatment was considered. This is not to suggest, however, that every attempt should not be made during the process of mobilization to enlist support even from potentially hostile groups. To define progress in terms of the state is not to deny the existence of smaller groups within the state. The effort shall be made to harness various group interests in order to make them part of an organic whole.

Operationally the best chances of success for the program lie in enlisting the support of the youth of the country and, of course, by the practical test of successful government since mobilization is inevitably accompanied by rising needs and expectations, which must not be frustrated if stability is to be preserved. It is for this last reason that exaggerated claims for economic benefits cannot be made since it is more than likely that a period of austerity would precede prosperity. If values are defined primarily in social terms – against race and class prejudices, in favor of self-sacrifice – then the probability of surviving the transitional period of reform is greater.

It has been contended in some quarters that the postulation of new goals in society requires of necessity that the old institutions be scrapped. This is an extreme position even though some institutional arrangements might have to be modified. No matter how rapid and thorough a change is effected some element of continuity with the past must be preserved because of certain psychological implications. To go rapidly and yet not to appear to do so is tactically the wisest approach. The Parliamentary Constitution is the best example which can be considered. If the Constitution is so castrated that it can perform no useful function, then it must be radically transformed. It is to be hoped, however, that any constitution in the area will have sufficient flexibility to serve the ends of the new elite.

Earlier it was stated that strong central government need not exclude popular participation, and this can now be considered further. The government would be supported either by a formalized political party or by organized elements in the community. In the former case the party structure should be such as to allow the free upward flow of ideas. One danger to be guarded against in a poor community such as ours is that a party may tend to accept financial support from certain interests in the community, which is the surest way of betraying the popular cause. In the second case, arrangements can be made on a regional basis so that a sense of identification is brought about by the people themselves carrying out local projects within the national framework. At the same time this would lessen the necessity for extensive bureaucratization.

In favor of the Civil Service, it must be said that this is one of the few credit entries in the colonial ledger. The West Indies is unique among territories on the eve of independence in being able to boast of a civil service that is almost completely local. These skills should be utilized, one field in which this is possible being that of specific planning. The caliber of individuals required on a planning staff must be no less than that of those required to take policy decisions. In fact, greater academic detachment is demanded of the planner. Gifted individuals in the society must always be wooed since their insights can be of great help in formulating policy. One is minded to cite C.L.R. James, whose contribution to Trinidad and the West Indies, has not been inconsiderable. It shall be the function of such individual thinkers, of the planner, and of the political leaders, constantly to reassess the national situation. Any system adopted must have within it the germ of change – it ought to be capable of transforming itself or even of being superseded without there being a bloody revolution. We cannot claim to guarantee this, but certainly, if democratic devices are built into the system, then when the new equilibrium is achieved following on the social revolution, the stage will be set for internal democratization.

Dr. Walter Rodney was a Professor of History at the University of the West Indies, Mona, Jamaica and at the University of Guyana. He was also a member of the WPA (Working Peoples Alliance) in Guyana. He was assassinated in Guyana in 1980.

Earl Augustus was a close friend of Dr. Walter Rodney from the time when they both attended The University of the West Indies, Mona in the 1960's. Back home in Trinidad and Tobago, Augustus became part of the struggle on behalf of the Trade Union Movement.

## 13 ECONOMIC INTEGRATION IN CENTRAL AMERICA

By John W. Crow

*Reprinted from Finance and Development Vol:III, Number I, March 1966*

(Taken from Flambeau, Number 9, July 1968)

In various parts of the world, groups of countries hope to achieve more rapid development through regional economic cooperation leading to eventual economic integration. Experience shows, however, that even in the most favorable circumstances the economic unification of sovereign states is an extremely arduous and complex process. The Central American Integration Program is no exception. While notable progress has been made, many problems need to be resolved before the goal of full economic union can be achieved.

While the movement toward Central American unification that has taken place over the last few years constitutes a new departure, it has deep historical roots in what has been termed "the Central American tradition." This is the conviction shared by many Central Americans for more than a century that there exists among their countries a community of interest which transcends political and economic divisions and rivalries.

Although the five Central American nations (Costa Rica, El Salvador, Guatemala, Honduras and Nicaragua) were included as provinces in a single administrative unit for most of the Spanish colonial era, the individual communities scattered down the length of the mountainous isthmus enjoyed a good deal of independence. Therefore, in the early 1820s, when Spanish rule crumbled, its substitution by a united Central American nation was only one of a number of possibilities. In the next two decades attempts were made to establish a federal form of government for the whole region, the United Provinces of Central America, but local rivalries and separatist tendencies proved too strong and by 1840 the five nations had emerged as independent entities.

The collapse of the attempts at federation did not, however, mean that the aspiration toward Central American political union was discarded; in later years, many attempts were made to achieve this goal. All were signally unsuccessful. Although the ideal of a Central American community rising above local divisions was widespread, it was never able to prevail over the short-term demands of practical politics. In the first place, the smaller nations were profoundly suspicious of the ambitions of their larger neighbors. Secondly, agreements between nations often broke down through lack of a consensus at home. It became increasingly clear that immediate political union was not a practical aim. A new approach was needed.

By the beginning of this century many supporters of union had come to realize that the key lay in a gradual approach stressing regional cooperation in specific fields of common interest rather than in general political agreements Only after World War II, however, when economic development and integration became matters of worldwide concern and investigation, did a blueprint for cooperation become available which could, on its own merits, attract and sustain the interest of individual governments. This interest soon led to the formulation of the Central American Economic Integration Program.

## THE PREPARATORY STAGE

At the Fourth Session of the United Nations Economic Commission for Latin America (ECLA) in June 1951, the Central American representatives introduced an important resolution. In this resolution they "expressed the interest of their governments in the development of agricultural and industrial production and of transportation systems in their respective countries so as to promote the integration of their economies and the expansion of markets by the exchange of their products, the coordination of their development programs and the establishment of enterprises in which all or some of these countries have an interest."

This was a fresh start which made it clear that the Central Americans aimed at nothing less than the achievement of full economic integration – but also, for the present, nothing more. This declaration of policy was followed a few months later by the signing of the Charter establishing the Organization of Central American States, a body designed to serve as a political forum for sovereign nations whose principal instrument was to be periodic meetings of the Ministers of Foreign Affairs. The preamble to its Charter reveals the new gradual approach: "the procedure tried in the independent life of the Central American Republics for restoration of their former unity have proven ineffective and....modern international law offers adequate formulas for this end through the institution of regional associations." Finally, in August 1952, the five Ministers of Economy met to establish the Central American

Economic Cooperation Committee, to which was entrusted the task of directing the future programs of the economic integration movement.

The committee was faced by a most challenging situation. In spite of their historic sense of unity, the Central American States, in the middle of the twentieth century, traded little within the area – their trade with one another was only 5 per cent of their total trade. Yet from the very outset the Economic Cooperation Committee, whose Secretariat was provided by ECLA, saw its task to be the creation of a multilateral free trade area complemented by a program to stimulate industrialization throughout the region. It was considered that through the achievement of a common market in Central American goods the way would be opened for the establishment of industries which could function efficiently only on a regional scale. These industries, supplying a market of some 10 million people rather than small national markets (the largest of which at that time had fewer than 3 million) would, it was hoped, prove an important element in stimulating development and trade within the area. The pattern of industrial growth was to be based upon what has been termed the principle of reciprocity, that is to say the integration industries would have to be distributed evenly among the five nations.

The activities of the Economic Cooperation Committee over the first few years were devoted to carrying out studies in a large number of fields. These investigations, undertaken by specialized subcommittees, ECLA itself, and technical assistance missions from outside the area, were designed to provide information which could serve as a basis for adapting the integration formula to Central American circumstances. Among the subject studied were potential integration industries; agricultural development; road and maritime transportation; electric power; weights and measures; public administration; the effect of free trade on fiscal revenues; and the problems of development financing.

## First Results

The first concrete results of these activities were the establishment of two Central American institutions, the Advanced School of Public Administration (1954) and the Institute for Industrial Research and Technology (1956), and the adoption of each country of the Central American Uniform Customs Nomenclature. These were advances but they were only preparatory to the task of drafting a series of agreements through which the basic structure of the integration program, the free trade area, the system of integration industries, and the common external tariff could be brought into existence.

This work was begun in earnest in 1956 when the Economic Cooperation Committee made a formal request that ECLA and groups of country representative prepare draft agreements relating to multilateral free trade and integration industries. In June 1958, representatives of all five nations met to sign the final versions, the Multilateral Treaty on Free Trade and Economic Integration and the Agreement on a System of Central American Integration Industries. Work on agreement establishing a unified external tariff had been held back until these two basic agreements were signed.

## THE INSTRUMENTS OF INTEGRATION

In accordance with the gradual spirit of the Integration Program, the Multilateral Treaty provided for the creation of a free trade area within ten years of its entry into force and the establishment of a customs union "as soon as conditions are appropriate." As a first step in this direction, the Multilateral Treaty included a list of some 200 commodities on which all import and export duties and other similar charges would be eliminated immediately. The economic impact of this measure was, however, much smaller than might be thought. The free trade provisions were restricted by the Multilateral Treaty to natural products and manufactures of the contracting parties, but not many of the items included in this list were actually produced within the area at that time. In addition to the agreement on free trade in commodities, the Multilateral Treaty provided for national treatment in each country of the persons and investments of the other four.

The declared purpose of the Agreement on Integration Industries, signed on the same day as the Multilateral Treaty was "to promote the establishment of new industries and the specialization and expansion of existing industries within the framework of Central American integration," it was also to ensure that this would be done "on a reciprocal and equitable basis in order that each and every Central American state may progressively derive economic advantages." A Central American Industrial Integration Commission was set up to carry out the Agreement. The output of the designated industries would receive free entry into all five markets, while the same products of plants located in Central America but falling outside the system would gain free entry only after a ten year transition period during which the protective duty would be progressively reduced. The Agreement confined itself to the enunciation of general principles and left the details to the separate protocol required for each industry. Such a protocol would not only specify the type of industry and its country location but would also stipulate capacity, quality standards, the degree of participation of Central American capital, and the uniform tariff protecting the industry's products. Equitable distribution was obviously important, and among other measures to achieve this, it was agreed that no country could acquire a second integration industry until each of the five had been assigned one.

With the successful conclusion of negotiations in the fields of free trade and industrial policy, the Economic Cooperation Committee turned to the third key requirement of the integration program, the creation of a common external tariff. This was achieved in September 1959, when representatives of all five nations concluded the Central American Agreement on the Equalization of Import Charges. Tariff equalization was to be based on two commodity schedules, one to have immediate effect and to take effect progressively over a period of two to five years.

Thus, in the space of just over one year, the three basic aims of the integration program as originally conceived were translated into treaty commitments. However, even as this was occurring, doubts arose within Central America not only about the direction the integration movement was taking but also about the desirability of economic integration in any form. While the two agreements concerning free trade and industrial policy concluded in June 1958 had been signed by representatives of all five nations, not all the signatories, even by the end of 1959, had deposited the instrument of ratification. Only three ratifications were needed for the Multilateral Treaty to enter into force and these were on deposit by the middle of 1959, but for the more controversial integration industries agreement all five ratifications were required to make it effective. Only three had been obtained by the end of 1959, and it has become increasingly clear that there would, at the very least, be some considerable delay before all five ratifications were deposited. Important bodies of opinion in one of the countries were becoming more and more skeptical as to the benefits it might obtain from participation in the integration program. After seven years of progress following the fresh start in 1951, the prospects for Central American Integration were once more clouding over.

## REORGANIZATION AND REORIENTATION

Instead of allowing the entire program to flounder, three of the participants – El Salvador, Guatemala and Honduras – began intensive negotiations aimed at preserving as much as possible of the integration movement and even at giving it new impetus. The result of these deliberations was the signing in February 1960 of the Treaty of Economic Association. This tripartite Treaty, the first to be concluded without the sponsorship of the Economic Cooperation Committee, went much more directly about the business of creating a common market in Central American products. The Method adopted in the Multilateral Treaty was exactly reversed, in as much as the new Treaty granted immediate free trade status to all but a few specified natural and manufactured products of the member countries. Furthermore, trade in most of these remaining commodities was freed within five years. As in the September 1959 Agreement on the Equalization of Import Charges, the unification of external tariffs was to be achieved over a period of five years, but the new Treaty also foresaw the establishment of a common customs administration when all tariff rates had been standardized. The most radical innovations, however, were in the field of industrial policy. In the new integration system the regional industry concept was abandoned and its place taken by a Development and Assistance Fund to promote economic integration and development by "facilitating public and private investment for production purposes."

This burst of activity on the part of three of the five members stimulated a new approach. In April 1960 the 'Economic Cooperation Committee held a special meeting, at which all five countries were represented, to consider how the older agreements and the new tripartite Treaty of Economic Association could be reconciled. As a result of this meeting the Economic Cooperation Committee voted (with one abstention) to instruct its Secretariat to prepare a new draft treaty "for the accelerated integration of the five countries." Although the instructions did not make any explicit reference of the tripartite Treaty, the burden of these directives was that the draft should follow the general lines of that Treaty, but should also include the integration industries program.

## THE 1960 AGREEMENTS

The developments led directly to the signing, in December 1960, of the General Treaty for Central American Economic Integration and two related agreements, the Agreement to Establish the Central American Bank for Economic Integration and the Second Protocol to the Agreement on the Equalization of Import Charges. From that time up to the present this General Treaty has served as the basic instrument of the integration movement. Only four nations signed these agreements, but both the General Treaty and the Bank Agreement made explicit provision for the eventual accession of the fifth.

The General Treaty, following the timetable and procedures set out in the tripartite Treaty, called for the establishment of a common market not later than five years after its entry into force. To this end, the signatories agreed to conclude subsidiary agreements for the adoption of a uniform customs code and the necessary transport regulations. In addition to determining the trade system, the General Treaty provided for significant advances in the much debated area of industrial policy. The integration industries agreement signed in 1958 and still not in effect, was incorporated into the new Treaty, now with the additional provision that the first plants were to be chosen within six months. It was also agreed to harmonize fiscal incentives to industry.

To "direct the integration of the Central American economies and to coordinate policy," the Treaty created the Central American Economic Council to be composed of the Ministers of Economy of the contracting states, an Executive Council, and a Permanent Secretariat. The Economic Council, composed of the same members as the Central American Cooperation Committee was called upon to "facilitate the execution" of the latter's resolutions. Thus the task of guiding the evolution of the integration program became to a much greater degree than before the responsibility of purely Central American institutions.

The agreement on the Central American Bank of Economic Integration was signed the same day as the General Treaty. The Bank's title was meaningful; not only was it barred from making investments in industries of a purely local character, but it was specifically charged with seeking a "balanced economic development" of the member countries, implying a special effort to channel resources into the economically weaker members. The initial capital resources of the Bank were fixed at the equivalent of U.S. $16 million, payable in local currency.

### SUBSEQUENT DEVELOPMENTS

Since the end of 1960 the integration program has progressed along two distinct but complementary ways. The first way has been by giving effect to the provisions of the 1960 agreements, the second by pursuing new initiatives to carry Central America beyond these agreements toward full economic Union. An important development was the return of Costa Rica to the program in 1962, so that when the long range aspirations were set out in the Declaration of Central American heads of state on the occasion of President Kennedy's visit in March 1963, all five countries were once again involved.

## THE IMPLEMENTATION OF THE GENERAL TREATY

The General Treaty entered into effect in June 1961, thus setting June 1966 as the date by which the free trade area and the common external tariff are to be achieved. Subsidiary agreements on external tariff equalization were duly signed in July 1962, January 1963 and August 1964. Over 98 per cent of the total number of items included in the uniform customs nomenclature are now covered although the few items still pending, notably automotive vehicles, petroleum products, radios and television sets, and wheat flour, account for about 20 per cent of the region's imports. Furthermore, equalization of duties on these items could strongly affect import duty receipts, which yield approximately 40 per cent of the combined tax revenues of Central America.

The two agreements provided for by the General Treaty in the field of industrial policy, the Agreement on Fiscal Incentives for Industrial Development and the Protocol to the Agreement on a system of Central American Integration Industries were signed in July 1962 and January 1963 respectively. The Agreement on Fiscal Incentives aimed at introducing a greater degree of uniformity into the kinds of benefits – mainly in the form of tax relief – the various countries grant to industrial enterprises. The industries to receive benefits were divided into three groups according to priority.

The Protocol to the integration industries agreement created the first two such enterprises, a rubber tire and tube industry in Guatemala and a caustic soda and chlorinated insecticides industry in Nicaragua. In addition, it provided a new basis for regional industrial development, the Special System for the Promotion of Productive Activities. Industries which are established under this system receive the benefits of free trade and uniform tariff protection from the time production begins, provided that they have capacity to satisfy at least 50 per cent of regional demand. In sharp contrast to the integration industry regime, no provision is made for an even geographic distribution of the industries which might be set up under its terms.

While both these agreements were signed within about six months after the General Treaty's entry into effect, there has been considerable delay in ratifying them. The Fiscal Incentive Agreement calls for five ratifications, but only four have been deposited at the time of writing. For the Integration Industries Protocol, which required only three deposits, the third was not obtained until February 1965 – more than two years after the Agreement had been signed. This lag in ratifying the agreements on industrial policy is indicative of the concern of some countries that they may not receive an adequate share of new regional industry. It does not mean that any of the countries now have misgivings about economic integration as a goal.

## TOWARD ECONOMIC UNION

The most striking indication of the progress made by the integration movement is the dynamic rate of growth of intra-Central American trade. From 1951 to 1961 this commerce grew on average by 14 per cent a year, while over the period from 1961 to 1964 the annual increase jumped to over 40 per cent. Furthermore, this upsurge has been accompanied by an even greater increase in trade in industrial products, so that by 1964 such items accounted for almost 60 per cent of the value. Against such a background it is easy to understand the interest that has been shown in moving toward an even greater degree of unification than that provided for in the General Treaty.

Important steps in this direction were taken toward the end of 1961, when the Central American Bank for Economic Integration and an associated institution, the Central American Clearing House, began operations, which since then have expanded rapidly. CABAI, as the bank is usually known, acting as a funnel for official development capital from both within and without the area, has to date granted loans totaling over $30 million. Most of this sum has gone to private industry, but there are indications that in the future the bank will play an increasingly important role in financing public sector investment especially of a regional character. Future operations will be financed largely from the recently created Central American Integration Fund, a joint venture of the United States and Central America was $42 million. In 1964 payments made through the Clearing House, established with the aim of promoting the use of Central American currencies in transactions among member countries, was the equivalent of almost 75 per cent of intra-regional trade.

The task of coordinating national development planning efforts began in 1962, with the establishment of the Joint Programming Mission under the auspices of the Inter-American Development Bank, the Organization of American States, and ECLA. This body, in cooperation with the various national planning agencies, has produced a development plan for the period 1965-69 for each nation.

The successful operation of the Clearing House has inspired the various central banks to begin work on the establishment of the monetary union foreseen in the joint declaration of March 1963. In 1964 they concluded an agreement which provided for the eventual establishment of a monetary union through the gradual expansion of monetary and fiscal cooperation and coordination within the area. While the achievement of the final goal will undoubtedly take a considerable time, the fact that all five countries have liberal payments systems and stable exchange rates makes the task much easier than it might otherwise be.

These parallel strands of development began to be brought together in April 1965, when for the first time a joint meeting of the Ministers of Economy and the Ministers of Finance was held. This meeting was also attended by the presidents of the central banks and the directors of the national planning offices. After a discussion covering many aspects of both development and financial policy, namely economic planning activities and public investment policy and fiscal policy, a series of resolutions was adopted calling for further studies on a Central American level in some fields and the preparation of draft agreements by the Permanent Secretariat of the General Treaty in others. This meeting could mark the beginning of a new phase in Central American relations, one in which a distinction between economic and political decision is no longer appropriate.

## 14 THE FUTURE ROLE OF CARIBBEAN YOUTH

By   Kenneth John

(Taken from Flambeau, Number 9, July 1968)

The future role of Caribbean youth is obvious. It is to act as the prime lever of radical social change. In order to do this, youthful energies must be coordinated along three distinct but complementary fronts. They must aim at forging some sort of viable unification of the area; they must be directed to stimulate independent thinking; and they must set as a target the attainment of a meaningful national identity. These three goals do not fall into mutually exclusive categories and, in fact, it is suggested here that any one of them is the logical precondition of another. For example, as soon as one begins to think seriously of the West Indian situation, in short as soon as one applies independent thinking to the Caribbean problem, it would become clear that some form of association is sorely needed. And in order to make any association really live, one needs to give it a spiritual base which alone can be found in a national identity.

We must begin with the sobering fact that we have been the plaything of History. We are essentially an immigrant society of polyglot peoples. Several metropolitan powers balkanized the West Indies and so divided and ruled us that high-falutin notions such as Caribbean integration fell outside the breadth of our mental range. We were the tropical extensions of the "Mother County" and we preferred to remain that way, mirroring all the parent institutions to a fault and engaging in a pathetic display of empty mimicry. The area of effective political operation was narrowly circumscribed; the tie with Europe was unbreakable. The colonial situation had imposed serious limits to the political horizons of our predecessors. They did not try to weld us into a harmonious body for the simple reason that subtle indoctrination and acculturation, backed up by the ultimate possibility of the techniques of violence had taught them that peace on earth was assured only by toeing the colonial line. But the same excuses cannot be made for the passing generation. They saw the need for Caribbean unity and they had the opportunity to realize it, but they chose to ignore it. Or rather they paid a sort of ritualistic token deference to it in the half-baked attempt at a Federation which collapsed because they never had their heart and soul in it. This limited union which was established was a step in the right direction, but it folded up. And now the young people have been left with a feeling of hollowness and betrayal, with dashed hopes, frustrated aspirations and unfulfilled dreams. The monumental task is left the youth to salvage what they can from the wreckage of broken pledges, to ensure that a West Indian nation rises phoenix-like from the ashes of past failures; to give substance and form to the longings of our people whose deepest yearnings and innermost feelings clamor for a respected place among the comity of nations.

And by West Indian nation is not meant merely a federation of the English speaking territories. Such a proposal will smack of supreme arrogance. Why should we let the accident of colonial history clap on mental blinkers and chart the course of our future? It is specious reasoning to suggest that because Puerto Rico was culturally dominated by Spain then caught the fancy of the Americans, or that for one reason and another France had refused to swap Martinique and Guadeloupe at the international bargaining table, or that the Dutch found Surinam to their liking, or that a few of the other territories were conquered by, where they didn't lapse to, Britain that a seal has been set on the separate development of all of them. This would be a most retrograde action based on a false logic. It would be a tragic proposition in the context of a changing world of economic blocs, political unions and ideological camps which cut across linguistic barriers traverse cultural boundaries and often make nonsense of our imperial designs. Moreover, geography is very much on our side. A map of the West Indies shows that we are all neighbors. Martinique is sandwiched by St. Lucia and Dominica, Guadeloupe by Dominica and Montserrat. Puerto Rico is a convenient resting place between St. Kitts and Jamaica. Surinam is contiguous with Guyana. And so forth. It would seem that the impersonal forces are all conspiring to bring us together. All that is needed is a human agency to interpret the mood of the times, to capitalize on the objective circumstances, and to set in motion the necessary machinery to bring about closer association.

Admittedly there are many pitfalls and stumbling blocks to integration but they can all be surmounted on the single condition that we really want to overcome them. The ingrained selfishness, political ineptitude and provincialism which seem endemic to the region would disappear overnight if the right people assumed leadership simultaneously in the various units. But there are other bugbears which are much more difficult to remove. We have developed – if developed is the word – under different European countries which have tried to create us in their own images. This means that we often differ in our attitudes, political idiom, language, culture and social shibboleths. There is strength in adversity, provided that differences do not go so very far as to become unbridgeable. There must be a community of interest, some common platform, a spirit of togetherness which can inspire confidence in amalgamation. There must be broadly similar ideals, shared fundamental beliefs, and an honest approach to life which is the hallmark of an open mind. It so happens that in different societies these required bonds of fellowship will be more readily encountered among the youth than among the older folk steeped in the tradition of their respective societies. The youth, almost by definition, have not been completely inducted in their particular social system, overwhelmed by their immediate environment, nor mentally immersed in the prevailing ideology of the country. In other words, the youth would not have already accommodated themselves totally to their society and acquired the tricks of the trade which make for successful living in material terms, in their particular territories. They know that there are alternative routes and other approaches to most social questions. There is no smug complacency among them. In fact, they often seem to be a bit maladjusted and would welcome change. Above all, youth tend to be idealistic and to trust one another – the two pillars on which a fund of common understanding can be built, and on which a viable nation can be founded.

The youth therefore are well equipped to be the instrument of social change in traditional societies which have a built-in aversion to change. The educational level of our typical society is extremely low but, if it could be measured, the thinking of the community will be discovered to be palpably lower. And that is where the youth must live up to its second assignment, that of stimulating thought. The bulk of our populations, including the formally educated segment are afflicted with a mode of thinking that is unscientific and pedestrian. For whereas science thrives on questioning and doubt and makes reservations for the uncertainties, randomness and element of change involved in most of its so-called conclusions, the pattern of our lives in these parts is the very antithesis, based as it is on dogma and authority. Our thinking is generally cast in iron mold and we seem to have pat, ready-made answers to all questions. Answers to ultimate questions can all be found by citing the relevant section of the Bible. The more urgent everyday political and economic issues can be settled by perusing a so-called authoritative text or, at the lower level, by browsing through Reader's Digest or Time Magazine. Youth needs to sponsor the scientific attitude in the application to local problems. Far too many of our conclusions are really conditioned responses to situations rather than the logical deduction which results from a critical analysis of the facts.

A catalog of things accepted as by an act of Faith would be too long to present here. One or two references will suffice. Take the question of Government participation in the economy. We have inherited as an absolute ethic of the colonial school that Government and business cannot mix. It is the classic concept of Government whose limited role is restricted to providing the economic infrastructure, education, health, roads, Post Offices, etc., but leaves the business field for the capitalist class. It is a negative notion of the traffic-policeman state that regulates but does not actively participate. In short the duty of Government is to hold the ring for the entrepreneurs to engage in their inglorious free-for-all. The proper attitude is not to swallow this concept hook, line and sinker, but to challenge this view which might be appropriate for other societies and/or earlier times. If we do this, we may discover that some of the traditional arguments used to shore up this laissez-faire philosophy are untenable in our circumstances and either persist as old habits or are deliberately sponsored by people who have something to gain from their operation. This is not an argument in favor of communism, socialism or any other ism for that matter, unless it be pragmatism – the philosophy of doing whatever is discovered to be best in the circumstances. But it is apparent that one of the brakes on our social progress stems from the fact that we have internalized certain largely irrelevant economic and political postulates which advocate an unqualified adherence to primitive capitalism, regardless of the costs. And there are a number of other institutions and beliefs which have been imposed on us and which we have accepted untested. In our own territory we have borrowed the British approach to politics which we strain to emulate and only end up in parodying. Following the advanced countries, we want to mechanize willy-nilly in the face of mounting unemployment. With a population explosion on our hands, we leave it to the Roman Catholics to lay down the rules respecting birth control. And so on. For reasons stated earlier, it is the youth who will have to bell these cats. Not because the elder people are afraid to bell the cats, but because in the scheme of things they don't even see any cats to bell. So completely are they enmeshed in the system.

I fully realize that the climate of opinion is hostile to anyone who wishes to subject these societies to rational analysis and come up with tentative answers. The people who have accommodated themselves to the status quo are allergic to any suggestion of change. They feel threatened. Anyone who has the temerity to parade evidences of an independent mind is sure to be accused of harboring dangerous unorthodoxies. Such folk may even be called subversives, which they are, depending on what you mean by the term. The paradox of the situation is that a dissident minority in the advanced countries are allowed to criticize their Government policy where such a luxury is not permitted their colonials. Examples abound. Robert Kennedy, Fulbright and Wayne Morse can oppose the scale of American operations in Vietnam, but the Communist label is pinned on any colonial critic. A number of Americans are distressed by the deplorable living conditions of "the other America" which spurn the race riots and condemn the squalor which has vomited up Stokely Carmichael and forged its own appropriate philosophy of Black Power. But Stokely Carmichael has been banned by the Government of Trinidad, the land of his birth. Beckford had his passport seized in Jamaica apparently because, like a number of his brother economists in the advanced countries, he saw something to praise in Castro's agricultural policy. Liberal thinkers all over the globe are advocating a demilitarization of the world, but Jamaica on attaining independence invited America to install military bases and Dominica has been used as a training ground for Canadian soldiers. Yet most West Indian intellectuals who expose these shortcomings of the society are deemed prohibited immigrants in neighboring territories and generally suffer a severe curtailment of personal freedom, all in the name of Democracy! But the nonconformist youth who have refused to play the game in the attempt to save their names from dry rot must be prepared to run these risks. For the alternative is more frightening – to spend a passive life, drifting with the tide, in a stagnating area that forms the back water of modern history.

A logical extension of independent thinking leads to the baffling question of a national identity – who are we, whence have we come, and whither are we going? As West Indians, we are desperately in need to some sense of identity which was lost in the historical nightmare that produced and left us with a pile of adjustment problems heaped high on our heads. Are we Dutch, French or English? Are we African, Indian or Chinese? Are we white, Black or Brown? Or are we simply a nondescript racial hybrid, a mongrel personality, a neutral character? As Hugh Springer has put it, "What is the essence of our West Indian-ness?" What is that indefinable quality that makes us peculiarly West Indian? It is mandatory that we possess an identity whereby we can calculate our bearing and plot the road ahead in this perplexing and topsy-turvy world. We need to rediscover ourselves probably by exhuming and examining our cultural roots in order to assume confidence, emotional stability and psychological balance. Again this is a job that can most efficiently be undertaken by the young people. For the most part, the ideas of our elders are already formulated and crystallized to the point of ossification. Their minds are irrevocably decided a particular way. They are closed. They would admit of no light. They have identified themselves with the Metropolitan power. Europe is their mecca.

    In the West Indies, there has been little movement in quest of an identity. This is mainly because our opinion leaders have been deluded into thinking that we do already possess a determinate identity which in reality is but a distorted reflection of the cruder aspect of the Western approach to life. The fact is that a hierarchy of Western social values has been superimposed on a people whose diverse backgrounds are not equipped to accommodate them. The society that results has a split personality and is monstrously artificial. The ordinary West Indian is ashamed of his "Pidgin English," which he helped to fashion by injecting strong doses of Africanisms into standard English, and in so-called elite company often tries to speak an immaculate clipped English to disastrous effect. St. Lucians often would not converse with a stranger in Patois because they have been taught that type of speech is an index of social standing and patois is the communication media of the lower class. A West Indian would rather serve tinned apple juice for dessert rather than a fresh tropical fruit. Rather than dress casually to meet the demands of an ennervating climate, West Indians prefer formal wear to meet the more exacting demands of a European oriented society. Some ten years ago you would not be admitted upstairs in a Vincentian cinema unless you wore a coat and a tie. Six years ago in Jamaica, the Minister of Education dressed in a guayabero, went to meet his Premier at the airport one steamy Sunday afternoon. For weeks after, the Press was flooded with letters denouncing the poor taste of the Minister. A member of the clergy in Trinidad, a Father Hendy, played carnival and thereby created a great furor in the calypso isle. And in most of the West Indian islands the native calypso is banned from radio stations during Lent! Barbadians were alarmed at the bombast of the Government in prohibiting fireworks on Guy Fawkes Night but transferred the celebrations to Independence Day a few days later. Immediately on attaining statehood, a constitutional status that is supposed to take us one more remove from the British Crown, the Police Forces in all the territories were named "The Royal Police Forces." Vincentians were shocked when two well-meaning persons started a program known as "Old Time Story" featuring local incidents taken from our rich storehouse of folklore! They want "Life with the Lions" instead. The practices of our established orthodox churches and the general approach of institutionalized religion are so formally European in orientation that "native" churches are beginning to appear in the form of so-called "Wayside religions" – pocomania, shakers and the rest – to cater for the spiritual needs of the social outcasts and the alienated. Above all a very high premium is set on the White face and the fair skin communities that are predominantly black.

The youth will have to attempt to set the record straight in all of these areas and more. Efforts must be made to stimulate spiritual, in a non-religious sense, development. The crass materialism and plantation mentality of slave society where everything was measured in terms of profit and loss still dog us. In every community, in every age the ruling class has always been the pace setter of the style of living and the determinant of culture patterns. In slave society, the slaves took the cue from their degenerate masters – the Barbarian community in the words of Shirley Gordon – and aspired to the unrefined life of the idle rich which they lived. The legacy left us is a community that is anti-intellectual to the bone, where poetry and other forms of literary expression can find little outlet, and where a native theatre has not been allowed to flourish and, in some places, not encouraged to evolve. Reading is considered a luxury and the various art forms, particularly creative dancing, are regarded as vulgar, thus leaving the nobler instincts of West Indian man blunted and underdeveloped.

The incisive question to which West Indians must present an answer is this: to whom must we turn for spiritual sustenance? Must we follow the movement of negritude as spelled out by Senghor and Cesaire? Or must we in every sense remain apron-stringed to our European owners? The dilemma is real and was beautifully dramatized in verse by Jamaican poet, Claude Mackay:

> "For the dim regions where my fathers came
> My spirit bondaged by the body, longs.
> Words felt, but never heard, my lips would frame,
> My soul would sing forgotten jungle songs.
> I would go back to darkness and to peace.
> But the great western world holds me in fee,
> And I may never hope for full release
> While to its alien gods I bend my knee."

Ours is a novel experience and it seems that we will have to fall back on our own resources and create the image which we think is appropriate for us to project. Youth may not have all the answers, but at least they recognize that there are questions to be answered. Time is fast running out and we will have to move – NOW. One is not advocating a so-called cultural revolution, Red-Guards style, but surely there are a number of areas in our respective societies crying out for change. But in this age of iconoclasm we must tread carefully. We must see that we do not throw out the baby with the bath water! There may be some things in the old order that merit preservation. We should endeavor to weave selected strands of the old and the new, blending what is good from Africa and Asia with that of Europe and evolve some sort of viable cultural syncretism. We should try and expose all issues to a free debate. Too many skeletons are rattling in the cupboards. And there is nothing so cleansing as a good, open fight. In our present circumstances silence is a luxury, conformity an indulgence. What form should our social structure take? What should our political philosophy be like? What shape should our economic system assume? How best to translate preachments about racial equality into an indisputable social fact. To these and other fundamental questions, the youth must address their minds.

**Dr Kenneth John holds a Ph.D. in Political Science from Manchester University. He is a newspaper columnist and a practicing lawyer in St Vincent and the Grenadines.**

## 15  THE DAY I SAW FORBES BURNHAM

By F. W. Dowers

(Taken from Flambeau, Number 9, July 1968)

Although I had never seen him, his name –Lynden Forbes Sampson Burnham – Guyana's Prime Minister – was familiar to me. Today, February 21, he was to address the Opening Session of a Conference of Commonwealth Caribbean Trade Ministers and their advisers, who were about to begin deliberations towards the setting up of CARIFTA, a Commonwealth Caribbean Free Trade Pact.

I sat in the Press Box in the ornate Parliament Chamber of the Guyana Public Buildings and awaited his arrival with restless anticipation. At 9:35 a.m., five minutes after the scheduled starting time, Forbes Lynden Sampson Burnham was ushered in. He was sandwiched between two top Government Officials, but though he was in the middle it was not difficult to detect who was the boss, the leader.

Burnham's face bore a calm and serene expression. His parted lips projected a friendly smile which bade hello and welcome to all. His dress was immaculate and his appearance suave, his hair was well groomed. His carriage was erect and stately, yet there was no trace of haughtiness. He took his position at the head of the Conference table facing the public address system, hardly aware that the whole house had stood to him spontaneously.

Lynden Forbes Sampson Burnham addressed the gathering in a voice that was dignified, yet cordial and inviting. He called the delegates from the nine other territories "fellow West Indians," "brothers." He pleaded for greater West Indian unity and prayed for the success of the conference.

When Burnham sat, a thunderous applause rocked the solid Italian-designed building. Even hardboiled pressmen, long immersed in reporters' protocol, spellbound by his speech, broke tradition and applauded.

In replying, the various delegations praised the Guyanese hospitality. They praised the Prime Minister for his achievements and those of his country under his administration.

When I left the Guyana Parliament Chamber, Forbes Lynden Sampson Burnham was being introduced to the visiting delegates during a short adjournment after the opening session; but Forbes Burnham needs no introduction to the visitor to Guyana. He has won the hearts of the Guyanese people; he has cast a spell on the peoples of the Commonwealth Caribbean, and has done the negro recently released from the shackles of slavery, justly proud. For here is a statesman among statesmen and a political Sampson on the vast South American continent.

**F. W. Dowers is a retired civil servant and presently resides in St. Vincent and the Grenadines.**

## 16  THE CHILDREN OF SISYPHUS: A REVIEW

By Karl John

(Taken from Flambeau, Number 1, June 1965)

The Children of Sisyphus by Orlando Patterson is the most interesting first novel by a Jamaican to appear on the literary scene since Vic Reid's "The Leopard". Reid's novel had its setting in Africa. Patterson writes of Jamaica. Not the Jamaica of North Coast tourist resorts and mansions on rocky hillsides – but the Jamaica of the West Kingston slums, the Dungle and its Denizens. These are the people in this novel who are real, who have substance, and people from the world outside – the world of vacuum cleaners and eggs – appear as shadowy figures – representative of a world that is unreachable even in dreams.

For some reason, this novel had made little impact on the Eastern Caribbean. Perhaps it is because West Indians have found very little of value in much of contemporary West Indian literature, and so are very disinclined to greet a new face with any enthusiasm.

This is a story about a people hopelessly trapped in an environment from which there is no escape. The Dungle is not merely a place, it is a way of life. To try to escape would be as futile as wishing to turn white.

Dinah, the character around whom the story is woven, leaves the Dungle. Her search for an identity, for an existence in the world outside, takes her to live with Alphanso, a policeman, to work in middle class suburbia with Mrs. Watkins and finally to the "Revival Zion Baptist of God" church-Shaker-type religion full of hell fire and repentance. Here she takes the fancy of Shepherd John, the Leader of the flock. The Shepherd is killed by the Elder Mother whose protégé and lover he had been. And blame for the deed falling on Dinah, she is literally torn to shreds by the flock in a scene to which only a Hollywood Horror Movie could do justice. Half dead, Dinah flees back to the Dungle whose tentacles have never released her. She dies there. There is never any doubt that the Dungle would reclaim her.

Most of all, this is the story of the Rastafarians, people living in a hopeless limbo, angry, baffled, spinning fantasies of a place in the sun far removed from Jamaica, but not even attempting to think of practical means to reach this Utopia. The Rastas are, in the eyes of Middle Class Jamaicans and white expatriates, an anachronism, a blot, an irritating canker on an otherwise pleasant paradise, of value only to the Sunday Social Workers in search of an M.B.E. And what does the Rasta think of himself? What does he think of the rest of Jamaican Society? Patterson's treatment of this Jamaican social problem reveals a rare sympathy, insight and much cynicism.

Without doubt, one of the most powerful characters in the novel is Brother Solomon – the Rastafarian Leader – a former Anglican priest. If something of the author's personal philosophy is present in the novel we will find it in Brother Solomon. He is a queer mixture of Existentialist Escapist, Nihilist. He deceives his trusting Rasta brothers in believing that the time of their repatriation is imminent. When the bubble burst, he calmly commits suicide. But why the deception in the first place? Because, he says, man is made to suffer simply because he is man, "The moment I overcome misery is the moment it conquers me". And after this there is only death, the final experience – "only the desperately poor and the rotten rich have searched for the meaning and could not find it; for the desperately poor, there is only the dreary circle going round and round."

And the justification for this act of betrayal? No man can live without hope. The Brethren, as yet unaware of the deception, have twelve hours of happiness. And what matters but the present?

Above all, this is a novel with no message for hope. Dinah's eventual death was mandatory. Just as the Rasta's failure to sail for Ethiopia was entirely predictable. Mary's violent death was punishment for daring to hope that, even by prostitution, she could earn enough to send her little Rosette to school, get her good food and clothes, enable her to "mix with brown people pickney."

The only escape for the Rasta lies in continuing the make-believe. Insulating himself from the world of Babylon. Convincing himself from the world of Babylon. Convincing himself that this life in the Dungle is but a temporary punishment for his sins. To make this feasible, he speaks differently, refuses to work for the white man, his eyes firmly fixed on his repatriation, his place in the sun.

Naturally, this first novel has its defects. The use of dialect is clumsy in parts. The author was apparently determined to bring something of contemporary Jamaican politics into the novel at all costs, hence the appearance of the thinly veiled popular Jamaican political leader in a carelessly contrived scene which does not fit convincingly into the narrative.

With its freshness and scope, the good things which can be said of the novel by far outway any adverse criticisms which can be made. We hope we can regard it as but a delightful hors d'oeuvre from Mr. Patterson.

**Karl John is a retired civil servant and was, for many years, Director of Planning in St. Vincent. He presently resides in St. Vincent and the Grenadines.**

# 17  SOME ASPECTS OF SCIENTIFIC PHILOSOPHY

By Baldwin King

(Taken from Flambeau, Number 1, June 1965)

In attempting to introduce the somewhat abstract and perhaps abstruse subject of scientific philosophy, I have two things to do. Firstly, I shall try to define the terms "science" and "philosophy" and hence indicate what may be studied in "Scientific Philosophy." Secondly, I shall select a problem or two and examine them for what they are worth.

Let us see what Bertrand Russell – one of the 20$^{th}$ century's most outstanding philosophers – has to say about science and philosophy.

"Philosophy consists of speculations about matters where exact knowledge is not yet possible. Roughly the difference between philosophy and science is that science is what we know and philosophy is what we don't know. Questions are perpetually passing over from philosophy into science as knowledge advances; that is, when something is established and discovered it ceases to be philosophy and becomes science.........One use of philosophy is to keep alive speculations about things that are not yet amenable to scientific knowledge; after all, scientific knowledge covers a very small part of the things that interest mankind and ought to interest them."

Here is another point of view by Ann Freemantle in her introduction to "The Age of Belief":

"The distinction between philosophy and science which also is a search after knowledge is basically the distinction between a point of view stemming from the general and one stemming from the particular. Science deals with some particular portion or aspect of reality arbitrarily abstracted from the whole by the human mind. Philosophy is concerned with the whole problem of what being is, of whether the universe is caused or is self-explanatory, and with the totality of phenomena in so far as they contribute to explain such fundamental problems."

I believe Bertrand Russell is using the word science in its most general sense to mean knowledge (Latin-Scientia). I shall use the word, however to mean that highly systemized body of knowledge built up by the application of the scientific method. The question arises, "What constitutes the scientific method?" What differentiates it from other methods of investigation? I can offer only simple and necessarily scrappy answers to such questions in a paper of this kind.

The basis of any investigation, whether scientific or not, is observation. Perhaps in science this observation is of a more meticulous, detailed and often quantitative type. The results of these observations provide much of the "data" of the inquiry, some of which is obtained by the use of instruments which aid the senses considerably.

The next stage is the setting up of experiments to examine the problem under controlled and reproducible conditions. Here we ignore the philosophical point of view that every event is unique in time and space and not observable again. Rather, we adopt the practical viewpoint that events and situations can be repeated, in a manner of speaking. It is then possible to keep certain factors in a given experiment constant and investigate the pattern of change of one factor resulting from a change in another factor. This, I think, is one characteristic the physical sciences possess which is not shared by other "sciences" like psychology and sociology.

Situations and events are often very complex and complicated. Even the so-called simple things often turn out on closer examination not to be so simple after all. As a result, a very potent method of tackling the problem is to break up the idealization into a number of parts for separate treatment. This is the idea behind "analysis," which is fundamental to scientific method. This step implies a simplification of the problem by treating the parts as if they were almost independent of each other. Scientists for some reason or other have an implicit faith in simplicity and if there happens to be a toss-up between two things it is customary to accept the simpler, within limits of course. Some authorities argue that analysis and simplification distort reality; others say no. However long the controversy continues, analysis will remain a necessary part of the paraphernalia of science.

The next stage in the scientific method is the construction of hypotheses and theories. Now there is a technical difference between a hypothesis and a theory, representing stages in the evolution of a scientific law. However, the two are often used interchangeably and we shall resort to this vagueness. The essential idea behind an hypothesis is that it tentatively tries to explain the results of a scientific investigation. Sometimes it is nothing more than a generalization of the observations. Some hypotheses or trial ideas are more plausible than others and if two or more hypotheses are advanced to explain the same set of facts, the simpler and more plausible is usually accepted.

The basic method of science is necessarily generalization or induction. This is the process of drawing conclusion about a whole class from observations on a few of its members, or as is often stated, reasoning from the particular to the general. In spite of the difficulty of justifying it philosophically, it is the method of reasoning commonly used in everyday situations (for example, when a man concludes that women are fickle, etc. from observation of a few women).

Closely related to induction is the deductive or logical method of reasoning which is used to arrive at certain conclusions starting from the postulated hypothesis. This is, in fact, the reverse of induction and consists of reasoning from the general to the particular. (All men are mortal; Socrates is a man, therefore Socrates is mortal.) If the first generalization or premise in the syllogism quoted is true to fact, the conclusion may or may not be true to fact depending on the truth or falsity of the second premise. The reverse can also happen. Let us for example apply the same syllogistic argument to Christ (All men are mortal; Christ is a man, therefore Christ is mortal.) Most Christians, I suppose, would question the truth of the conclusion – Christ is mortal – and if they agree with the premise – Christ is a man – they can only reconcile the two logically by asserting that not all men are mortal.

At this stage, scientists resort to the testing of their hypothesis and deduction by carrying out new observations or by conducting new experiments. What I have said earlier about the possibility of operating under controlled conditions has special relevance here. The testing of hypotheses is often regarded by the conceited scientist as one of the distinguishing features of scientific method. This attitude tends to antagonize other "scientists" like the social scientist who finds it difficult to restrict his investigations to the laboratory and so eliminate outside influences but who would argue most vehemently to get his discipline recognized as a science. (This, I venture to suggest, is a reflection of the powerfulness and reliability of the scientific method). In my own view, the quarrel is a fruitless one since it usually involves a re-definition of terms. What matters is the validity and usefulness of the results in aiding man in his struggle to better himself.

The final stage in the method of science is the evolution of the hypothesis, which has stood the test of time, into a scientific law. The word "law" is so often misused and misunderstood that I shall return to try to analyze the nature of scientific laws.

One of the recognized tasks of philosophy is to analyze the nature and structure of knowledge, so that one interpretation of scientific philosophy is the analysis of the nature and structure of scientific knowledge; perhaps a better description is philosophic science. This is my main interest in this paper. However, scientific philosophy may be taken to mean philosophy employing the scientific method. This, some will argue, is a contradiction in terms. How can scientific method, which includes experimenting and testing of hypotheses, be used in philosophy, a speculative study? This is a valid argument and, therefore, we are forced to conclude that the term is used rather loosely to mean the logical-analytical method in pure philosophy. In an effort to cater for various interests, I shall consider one question from each discipline.

Let us now look at the physical laws more closely. A law has been described by some authorities as a "true sentence which is general, spatially and temporally unrestricted, non-accidental and describing regularities". I interpret the word "true" to mean, of objects and situations, conforming to fact and reality. I shall not confuse the matter further by asking what constitutes reality, although this a valid and well-worn philosophical question. (For example, the idealist tradition represented by Francis H. Bradley, considers that all reality is mental or spiritual and that nothing can exist unless it either knows or is known. The French mathematician-philosopher Rene Descartes held the view that his world consisted only of himself and his thoughts). Suffice it to say that objects and events are real and that the exact nature of physical reality is immaterial to our present argument.

I would like to examine the statement that a law is a true sentence. Take the often-quoted law of common sense that "all men are mortal". The sentence is a generalization of observations made over a considerable period of time and all evidence supports the conclusion that all men are mortal. But what of the men who will be born tomorrow? Will they turn out to be mortal? Of this we cannot be absolutely sure. (For example, is it so fantastic to imagine that, should nuclear war ensue and man is irradiated excessively, drastic genetic changes may occur to make him immortal). However, men were mortal yesterday, they are today and there is no good reason to suspect they would not be tomorrow. It must be understood, however, that nothing can be true in the absolute sense since we can never know the "n th" case. This means, then, that when we use the word "true" to describe events, part of our meaning is that we are justified in asserting they are true within the context of things known. If one asks: "Is a common-sense law true (Are all men mortal?), he can usually be provided with a straight "yes" or "no" answer. Is the same thing possible with physical laws?

Physical laws are, in the generality, empirical and effectively summarize or generalize the results of some scientific investigation, requiring experimentation, etc. This feature, perhaps, distinguishes these laws from common-sense laws which usually have no scientific basis and which are "general judgments whose meaning is immediate." Physical laws however are "symbolic relationships" intelligible only to physical scientists. To illustrate, let us recall a law of physics which generalizes certain events familiar to everybody. This law goes by the name of Boyle's Law (after the English scientist Robert Boyle). It states that the volume of a definite quantity of gas at a definite temperature varies inversely as the pressure of the gas; that is to say, if you double the pressure on the gas you halve the volume and vice versa. Now the real situation you would observe is, for example, that you trap a certain amount of air in the barrel of your bicycle pump by keeping the piston in position A. This amount of space occupied by the gas is represented by, or taken to be, the volume of the gas (i.e., volume is a sign or symbol representing the reality of the enclosed space). Next in this position A, you observe that it is necessary to exert some effort to maintain the piston in position A. The symbol for this reality is pressure. Also you are carrying out your observations on the gas in a given state of warmth or coolness whose symbol is temperature. Finally you observe, after you have devised instruments to "measure" the volume, pressure and temperature of the gas that if you move the piston into position B such that the volume is halved, then the pressure on the piston is doubled at constant temperature. The experiment is repeated on a number of gases under different conditions of temperature and the results summarized in a "physical" law which shows the relationship existing between the symbols or abstractions – volume, pressure, temperature – and which can usually be written as a mathematical formula. One may be tempted to ask, Is Boyle's law true? It is difficult to give a straight "yes or no" answer to this question (contrast the case of a common-sense law). In fact the uncouth physical scientist will most likely exclaim, "what a stupid question!" A more appropriate question is – Do all gases behave the way Boyle's law suggests? The answer is no. Although gases tend to show some kind of regularity in behavior, the law is found to apply to all gases at sufficiently low pressures and high temperatures; at other pressures it applies at a given temperature to some gases only, whereas in some cases it does not apply at all. Therefore Boyle's law holds well only under certain conditions which one might call the boundary conditions, and to be really meaningful a statement of the boundary conditions must accompany a statement of the law.

One thing that must be clearly understood is that a physical law is usually not exact and all embracing. It must be approximate because of its very nature. In point of fact, it is not unusual to find more than one law or mathematical formula being put forward to summarize the same set of facts. Thus physical laws are neither true nor false and fortunately so, because scientists are just not interested in the truth of a law. What is of more immediate interest is whether the law is useful or not in controlling nature or predicting phenomena, which are among the aims of science.

Here is food for thought. Is the statement: "two and two equal four" true? My answer is that it is no truer than a physical law is true.

Let us now turn to a problem in philosophy – the nature of the external world. Bertrand Russell has a lot to say on this subject in Chapter 3 of his "Our Knowledge Of The External World". And what follows is essentially a summary of the first part of the chapter. Francis H. Bradley (1846 – 1924), whom we have met already as symbolizing the classical tradition, condemns almost all that makes up our everyday world – material things such as chairs and tables, space and time, the self etc. He insists it is impossible to talk about isolated events (e.g. the black wolf ate the stray sheep) because reality is an indivisible whole. The arguments he adduces to support this view are often highly complex and esoteric. Russell in fact, considers him as belonging to the universal skeptics "whose philosophy is as questionable as it is barren". Russell himself accepts the facts of sense and uses them as a starting point for philosophical inquiry and analysis.

Russell divides common knowledge of this kind into beliefs that are derivative and those that are primitive. That is to say, there are some things we only believe because of something else from which they have been inferred, while other things (for example, the facts of sense) are believed on their own account without the support of outside evidence. He goes on to distinguish between what he calls "hard data" and "soft data", hard data being defined as those which resist the "solvent" influence of critical reflection and soft data as those "which under the operation of this process, become to our minds more or less doubtful". He regards the facts of sense and the general truths of logic as the hardest of hard data and uses them to find out whether or not an external world exists.

According to Russell, the problem can take various forms. For example, "Can the existence of anything other than our own hard data, be inferred from the existence of those data"? Or "Can we know of the existence of any reality which is independent of ourselves"? In partial answer to the latter question, Russell points out that the question suffers from the ambiguity of the two words "independence" and "self" and attempts to interpret them. He claims that the only way in which one thing can be logically dependent on another is when the other is part of the one.

For example, the existence of a book is logically dependent on that of its pages – without pages, we cannot have a book. Again he suggests, among other things, two meanings of the "self" (a) the bare subject which thinks and is aware of objects and (b) the whole assemblage of things that will necessarily cease to exist if our lives came to an end. Concluding this bit of analysis, he says: " I think, however the self may be defined, it cannot be supposed to be part of the immediate objects of sense. Thus we must admit that we can know of the existence of realities independent of ourselves".

Russell has described himself as a logical atomist. He insists it is possible to break up knowledge into simple "atomic" propositions and then use logic to discover truth. Even with this approach, so many of his "proofs" seem to consist of nothing more than an extension or redefinition of terms to fit his conclusions. I suppose this could be excused, once we regard these philosophical questions merely as mental exercises. Proof of the existence of an external world comes under this category.

Here is yet another view which believes in objective reality: "When I judge, I judge that something is the case. If it is not the case, then I have misjudged and the allegation I have misjudged, implies that something else is the case. In saying that we think, we do not just signal what is going on in our heads; we describe or misdescribe reality".

My own belief is in an objective reality, that things have an existence all their own, that the chairs and tables and pens are there even when we are not perceiving them. However these things may appear differently to different people because of different physiology or perspective. Is it so difficult to imagine that when A looks at an object and sees what he calls a man, B looks at the same object and sees a mouse (what's in a word?).

This view of reality is a rather prosaic one, I will admit, but in the final analysis, if you are crossing the road when a car is proceeding down the road at a hundred miles per hour, will you happily stand there chanting Bradley quotes like "All reality is mental" or "Reality is an indivisible whole, etc"? No. You will get out of the way, fast.

**Dr Baldwin King is a chemical educator and researcher. He is presently Professor of Chemistry at Drew University, New Jersey, U.S.A.**

## 18     THE DEMOCRATIC PROCESS AND THE SINGLE PARTY IN THE NEW STATES

### By DANIEL WILLIAMS

(Taken from Flambeau, Number 1, June 1965)

As a rule, political institutions evolve mainly out of the social character of a country. The word "social" is used here to embrace all human activity and struggle within the state, and the culture that foments such activity. In spite of the evolutionary nature of these institutions it has been the practice to regard them as made to an approved plan, and to justify their beings. I call this the "post facto" approach and I do not consider it adequate since the arguments used keep assuming premises that were never contemplated.

The two-party state is considered the norm by the group of the West. They say that it is necessary for the preservation of democracy and the prevention of dictatorship. They say that there must be an organized opposition; and indeed in many quarters exposed to decades of colonialist thinking, to assert otherwise is almost treasonable. We in the West Indies have been overexposed to formulated thinking, and we have adopted an emotional attitude to this subject. We are afraid to examine it.

Let us look at the two party system in Britain, not forgetting that there is a small third party. This system in Britain reflects the class gradations that exist, and the division of the country into the "haves and the "have nots." The Conservative Party, officially called the Conservative and Unionist Party grew out of the Tory Party of the landed classes about the middle of the 19$^{th}$ century. Indeed, some of the "diehards" still remain and form the Right Wing of the Party, resistant to all change. The Labor Party is the political mirror of the working class movement which began to crystallize, after the Industrial Revolution dislocated large masses of urban labor. Landless, and divorced of the mechanics of production, they allied themselves with the Trade Union Movement and Cooperative Societies. Historically analyzed, the two party system in Britain grew out of the dichotomy of living standards of the people in a capitalist society based on the feudal tenure of land. The post facto argument justifies the inequality of standards between two opposing classes by saying this system is necessary for the proper functioning of democracy. The opposition, as the party outside the

Government is called, is indeed a true opposition. It represents a set of people who are opposed to the other set.

Out of this economic climate which nurtured the Labour party into the opposing party, ideological attitudes naturally developed. The Socialist theory, that the major industries and some of the land of the country should be under government control, is in fact the buttress against the other group, the Conservatives who believed that great wealth belonged to the few and that title and land and rank went hand in hand. The divergent ideologies were formulated out of an existing state of affairs, and those who speak of ideological differences as an argument for the two party state should bear in mind that the ideology is formulated by an actual state of affairs. Politically speaking, the reverse is hardly ever true in the state where the traditional pattern has been erased. It was before the Russian Revolution, when the wealthy and feudal Czars were overthrown, that the Marxist-Leninist theory of Communism was formulated on the experience of another country? Germany?

The Liberal Party sprang from the aristocratic Whigs of the 17$^{th}$ and 18$^{th}$ centuries. In the mid-19$^{th}$ century they represented the trading and manufacturing classes as opposed to the landed classes. They were the advocates of social reform. "The Party is supported by those of moderate incomes and by a lesser proportion of both rich and poor," says Michael Stewart. They are not normally a great force, although in the present precarious Labor Government in England they hold the balance of power.

Britain is a three-party State. However, the argument runs that the ideal state is the two-party state, since the Government must have an opposition to prevent abuse of power. But, every faction, every group in the country should, however, be free to form parties. And then there is instability like in France during the Third and Fourth Republics.

My thesis is that the single or the unified Party is the type of party best suited to the new underdeveloped independent states and the underdeveloped self governing countries seeking independence.

The one-party state reflects the image of the nation. The opposition to the one-party state was either the colonizer or still is the colonizer. Indeed, always it is the colonizer. It is also the group with entrenched positions, who prefer outside domination rather than control from within by their own nationals; the opportunist group, who either seek self-promotion or are the tools of an alien group who wishes to retain economic control by causing confusion within the nationalist ranks.

In the new independent states, and the near independent states, political autonomy is the means whereby these states can gain economic well-being. These countries are backward, having been used by the colonialist only as producers of raw materials for manufacture in the metropolitan state. This policy of extraction did not produce a local elite of technicians. The mass of the country is a laboring class. The elite is a class of shop clerks trained in simple interest and profit and loss. The super elite is the civil servant, the majority of whom are clerks and untrained for executive and administrative positions. The large masses of people belong to one class – the working class – whose chief industry near to independence and for some time after independence is agriculture. Industrialization in any measure comes long after independence when the metropolitan power cannot dictate the economic route of the raw material of wealth.

The priorities in such states are economic planning, education and social services. The best minds in such states are required to work together towards the national goals, which are primarily to raise the standard of living by training their citizens in industry and the technical skills of the modern age. Indeed, then, there is only one party, the party of exploited and underprivileged, the party of those who must unlearn the propaganda and the half truths of their colonialist training, and formulate a pattern of thinking indigenous to them, and appropriate to their unfortunate situation.

In such a situation, in such an emergency, who is the opposition, who is the other competitive party, and what is their role? If you accept that in the states under discussion, the economic philandering of the colonial powers created largely a class of laborers, mainly illiterate and wholly unthinking, where is the other party? If all are agreed on the national goals, what is the need for an opposition, except it be to obstruct?

Let us examine the composition of the probable opposition. Since the competitive two party system has emerged on what I shall call "the Lazarus/Divea line" with their innate ideologies, the opposition, or other party would comprise those who found their entrenched position under colonial rule threatened with the demise of colonialism. The planters who own large portions of the country, and who descend directly or otherwise from white overlords on sugar estates when sugar was an economic proposition are expected to form part of the other party, since the nationalist party must of necessity threaten their privileged position. But if the planters form no opposing Party, then who is this other party and from where does it emanate? This other party must, indeed, by the tool of the other group acting covertly. There is evidence that in some of these islands the planter group encourages the two party system by dividing the working class into two camps, aided and abetted by our own unscrupulous, but perhaps more correctly our more unthinking and naïve politicians. It is not unusual in some areas to see laboring people in the most straightened circumstances on opposing sides, completely unaware, as naturally they must be, of why they are opposing each other.

And so in the name of democracy the fratricidal struggle continues. The post facto argument, based on the excrescence of a feudal society – the two-party system – strangles and obliterates the national image.

But one must distinguish between the theory and the reality of practical democracy. The thesis that a single or unified party is best suited to the particular states discussed does not rule out freedom of speech within the single party; it does not condemn the right of discussion within the party. The single nationalist party must express the wishes of the majority of the masses of the people. The single nationalist party will and must depend on discussion to arrive at its decision. It is unnecessary in the states, and it is unnatural to have an organized opposition. I accept the definition by Madeira Keita of Mali of democracy. He says, "Democracy is the exercise of public authority in conformance with the will of the masses." The two party system is alien to the new states. Julius Nyere of Tanzania regards the African concept of "democracy" as similar to that of the ancient Greeks from whose language the word democracy originated. "To the Greeks," he says, democracy meant simply "government by discussion among equals." The people discussed and when they reached agreement the result was a "people's decision."

But even in Britain, in the time of national emergency there is a departure from the two party system and coalitions have been formed, that is to say, the country is run by a unified party. Wade and Phillips on "Constitutional Law" (6$^{th}$ edition at page 18) has this to say: "Of late years, the party system has not been working normally. National Governments composed of members of all or more than one of the major political parties have held office on five occasions since 1918. Their formation has been due to grave emergencies in foreign or economic affairs, which caused party differences to be sunk in the interests of national unity. However, inevitable and advantageous this form of government has been, it has resulted in depriving the House of Commons of an effective opposition ready to succeed the Government, and this has undoubtedly weakened the control of Parliament over the Executive. In 1945 the Government which was returned to power at the end of the war with Germany commanded so large a majority in the House of Commons that the role of the opposition was difficult to maintain; as a result of the general election of 1950 this majority declined to a mere handful...In theory neither very large nor very small majorities are favorable to the working of the two party system."

I find this statement apologetic. The writers concede the usefulness of the unified party which forms a National Government as opposed to a party Government in the time of emergency so that the best minds in the country can work together, but then laments that in such a situation the opposition dwindles into insignificance. They must have their opposition whether they need it or not. They must justify their iniquities of their social system by clinging to a form of government which in time of travail and tension they must discard. But must the new countries follow such tendentious reasoning?

The new independent state would have just won independence for the country. Whether it be the Tanganyika African National Union, the Convention People's Party, the People's National Movement or the Jamaican Labor Party, then that party becomes the nationalist party. How does an opposition emerge against the nationalist party at the very beginning of independence except it be constructed for an obstructional purpose? It may be that at the very beginning an opposition party based on ethnic origins may emerge, but then such an opposition is not the traditional opposition of which we were taught. It may be that gradually a true opposition may emerge based on ideological differences in the wide ambit of international politics.

But the usual opposition in these new states is a dissident power-conscious minority, a minority which is prepared to use subversive means to destroy the nationalist party. This is the group which provides the propaganda for the neo-colonialist and for international politics. In Ghana they tell you of the shackled opposition. In the Congo, with its plethora of parties, it is the cannibalism of a rebel government. For the group of the West, a Tshombe, but not an Nkrumah.

If the one-party state appears to be dictatorial it is only because of the manner in which a capitalist and hostile press is prepared to interpret the protective measures of the nationalist government against a minority which is not concerned with national goals. The duty of all government is to govern and to protect themselves from aggression from outside, as well as from within. Indeed, in these states the aggression is more insidious and oozes from inside. And since the aim of the truly nationalist government must be to raise standards of living and to make best use of its wealth, a thing which it was not allowed to do as a colonial state, clearly the intent of metropolitan power is still to retain economic domination of the new country as the Belgians have all too clearly shown in the Congo. Their duty, therefore, is to canvass for an opposition party within the state to disrupt nationalist planning, cause internal strife so that they may have good reason to return and continue to plunder the country. The case of Tanganyika is fresh on the mind. And Nyere had to call back the British and their troops.

The new independent state is the pawn in the game of international politics – the tug-of-war between East and West. The attempt by the colonial power to impose their pattern of party government on the new states, in circumstances completely different to those that exist in their country, is merely the method to ensure that the new states remain colonial in concepts and ideas. They have not hesitated to have a unified party when the emergency of the situation demanded it. The new states are a continuing emergency until they share in the prosperity of the present century and lead their people out of economic darkness. This emergency cannot afford the luxury of an organized opposition, be it paid or unpaid. The party is the government, and the party is the people. If the leaders are sincere, and their objectives are concerned with the liberation of the people from the forces of darkness, which the Imperialist made no effort to dispel, then there can be no true opposition. The loyalty which the citizen owes his nation is the loyalty which he owes not to any individual, but to the single party, the nationalist party which is the government.

The thesis is – and I accept the statements formulated by Von der Mehden, in his book "Politics Of The Developing Nations" that:

(a)   Political parties sabotage national unity.
(b)   Multiple parties waste valuable time and man-power.
(c)   The Western system of parliamentary party government does not fit local conditions.
(d)   Party competition is neither necessary nor natural.

For us newly independent or on the verge of independence, politics is the ethos of all our striving and aspirations for a better way of life, and for respect as a people in the world. It is the single image of a people not divided by schisms and class structures that we wish to present. Opposition is healthy if it is helpful, but that which seeks to destroy what has been created by years of working and waiting is malignant and must be contained. In these new countries the people are a single, unified party. The people are the party, the one party, the Government.

The one-party state is not necessarily dictatorial, and in any case dictatorship may be a product of either the one party system or the two-party system of Government. That is why, no doubt, Wade and Phillips say that neither very large majorities nor very small minorities are suitable to the working of the two-party governments. If the one-party state is undemocratic then the coalition government is also undemocratic. Certainly the democratic process is an attitude of mind rather than a political form. In Britain there are in fact great limitations to the pure theory of democracy. In the time of national crises and in the time of war individual freedom of movement and of speech are severely curtailed. Emergency regulations sometimes invest one man with an absolute discretion to decide who should be detained for security reasons; and there may be no appeal from the decision by the individual in such circumstances. Lord Atkin in a dissenting judgment in the case of Liversidge and Anderson is critical of such power, which nevertheless exists. Applying the theory of democracy to the realities of situations which may affect them adversely, the British through their Governors have declared states of emergency in many colonial territories. Practical democracy, therefore, is usually the tool of expediency.

Applying the same premise to the one-party state, it appears that in such a state, the majority must circumscribe the outer limits of the activity of the so-called opposition, whose existence seems of more import to the Western press than the existence of the Government itself.

The single party or the unified party seeks to cut across artificial social demarcations in the state and to hold the people together, so that the professional – whether he be lecturer, teacher, doctor, lawyer, engineer, or one of that brood of men who has been exposed to what is facetiously called "higher education" -- will form part of the single party in association with the peasant and laborer, and those who follow humble and menial duties to die more slowly than otherwise. And under this system, the Civil Service has no need to be neutral, since there is no organized opposition seeking a contradictory end. The Civil Service therefore is allied to the single party and subject to the disciplines of the party.

The colonialist teaching was designed to create division and dissension among the colonial people. It advocated a socio-economic class structure based on the bizarre and unnatural tabulation of human existence into middle, upper and lower classes. Illogically, the first class is always the middle one, the bourgeois – to which the supporters of this formula usually claim to belong. They never belong to the upper class, jetsam from the privileged positions of the landed gentry of the colonialist period. Most certainly they never belong to the lower class, that amorphous body of human debris which the economic mill ground into sub-humanity. It is to that class their forbears belonged, not them.

Competitive party politics divides the country into opposing camps. The new states with their lack of trained and skilled men, with their lack of professionals, cannot afford the luxury of genocidal competition in a two party system. On the evidence available, there is not the slightest justification for any new state, or any country approaching independence from the colonialists, to import all their political tenets, if, like the two party system, it is found to be completely alien to their natural philosophy and their local conditions. More so, when on examination it is found that the two-party system creates opposition to national aims, hampers progress rather than stimulates it, and divides the people rather than unites them, it should be abandoned.

**Daniel Williams practiced law in St Vincent and the Grenadines. He died in a tragic car accident in St. Vincent in 1971.**

## 19     HE DEFENDED EURO-AMERICAN IMPERIALISM AND EXPLOITATION

By Kerwyn L. Morris

(Taken from Flambeau, Number 1, June 1965)

[Editorial Note: In December 1964 the "Vincentian" published a letter on events in the Congo by one Mr. Spanel entitled, "They defend Cannibalism and Genocide." Kerwyn Morris, a Vincentian studying in Canada, was irked by what he considered the anti-negro bias and one-sidedness of the whole exercise, and he wrote a reply to the "Vincentian" that went unpublished. We thought that it might be a fine gesture if we put Kerwyn's article between our covers. This does not mean that we agree with all that Kerwyn has to say, just as, we hope, the editorial staff of the "Vincentian" did not imbibe most of what Mr. Spanel had to offer. It is essentially the view of an individual, but we publish it all the same. For we believe that it is only by a clash of opposing views that sparks of truth might fly out.]

The white brothers have joined hands once again in an attempt to re-enter Black Africa. History will forever repeat itself. This time they seek entrance by the back door, but with the same age-old tactics – the tactics of using the very black man to exploit his black neighbor. They did it centuries ago all over Black Africa when the slave trade was in full swing. They established ready alliances – war-like alliances with firearms in order to produce their highly perishable goods (human beings) for the "Middle Passage." It is estimated that this trade cost Black Africa some fifty million lives.

Here was the beginning of capitalist expansion by the very forefathers of those who today claim to be the vanguard of freedom and democracy; a beginning stained with the blood of millions of innocent Africans who perished helplessly as a means to the white man's ends. This stain shall last forever as a curse on those of the white race, and it is with this bloody discredit (for which they seem to have no sense of shame) that they continue their exploitation of Africa.

Mr. Spanel, by the very nature of his racial origin and by his association with American private enterprise, is bound to be oblivious of the above facts, for exploitation, be it of human or natural resources, is the very foundation of all corporations. This not being enough, he exposes his ignorance of African history. One should assess his article for what it is worth – practically nothing – and not be misled into associating its length and content with the position that he holds.

Mr. Spanel begins his article by referring to the "naked savagery in the Congo." May I ask him what he calls the Sharpeville shootings, the French atrocities in the Algerian war of Independence, the police handling of Negro demonstrators in the U.S.A. to name but a few acts of real savagery in this century? The white man should be the last one on the face of this earth to utter the word savagery. What was King Leopold I doing in "his" Congo but the very same thing that the Belgian paratroopers did not very long ago. Was there anyone to raise the cries of humanitarianism at that time? What were the cries of your forefathers then? I can tell you, Mr. Spanel: they were "kill every nigger on sight," "an arm or a leg for every round of ammunition wasted." The former was the cry that the Boers were using in South Africa to commit **their** genocide against the bushmen and the Hottentots, and the latter was Leopold's slogan that brought him his fortune in the Congo. The boot was then on the white man's foot, but whenever it is on the black man's foot, we hear different cries. We hear the cries, "save us," "innocent missionaries," "massacres," "genocide," and a host of others. Who raised the cries for the fifty million African souls lost in slavery through your greed, Mr. Spanel? Who raised the cries when Europeans were acquiring their African colonies with firearms? Who raised the cries for the poor Caribs that Mr. Duncan calls "the enemy?" Where were the humanitarians then? Where were your forefathers, Mr. Spanel? They were right there too, but they themselves were the very savages so you may not see them.

Mr. Spanel goes on to say, "Can it be that Western man with all his cultures and code of ethics...: Where are these culture traits and ethical codes to be found? I am afraid, Mr. Spanel, that they are found only in the form of the written word; but do you by any chance mean the idolatry of money worship as a positive culture trait and racial discrimination as an ethical code?

"The issue is not political or military. It is primarily moral," says the goodly gentleman. It is a moral issue in that for eighty years, a ruthless Belgian rule had shut off the Congo from prying eyes, and in that the extent to which Belgium (a member of the same Western club with all that culture and code of ethics in the world) had decorated its colonial ambitions with claims to the advance of civilization, had been exposed.

Contrary to what he asserts, the issue is both political and military. On July 11, 1961, less than two weeks after the Congo gained its independence, M. Tshombe, then Provincial President of Katanga, declared his province independent. He was supported to the hilt by the Belgians in Elizabethville and the Union Miniere, the company controlling the rich copper mines of the province M. Tshombe's regime depended then as it does now on Belgian arms, men and money. He was making it possible to realize the life dreams of Messrs. Verwoed, Salazar and Welensky, who had hoped to see a strong white-supremacist bloc in Africa comprising the Congo, South Africa, Angola, Mozambique and the short-lived Central African Federation of Northern and Southern Rhodesia and Nyasaland. The realization of such a bloc could never have been the result of that dear principle of one man one vote; a principle of which the Western powers boast for their countries, but not for their colonies. Where then are the political values implied by the use of the word democracy, Mr. Spanel? Are the Western powers not the guardians of these also?

Another political aspect is the entry of the cold war into that continent. Africa is a developing continent and cold war politics can serve it no useful purpose. Assuming that you also believe in the concept of self-determination, then Africa should be left free to develop along its own chosen path, regardless of what path may be chosen. The African leaders must decide for themselves, and not you or anyone else for them. Africa does not want to be dominated by any foreign power, be it Eastern or Western. The very "stooge regime" of which you speak is precisely what they do not want set up. They will be stooges of neither East nor West, nor will they be "poisoned by propaganda from either camp".

The military issue lies in the realm of power politics and the shifting balance of world power. As you said, and quite rightly too, "whatever the disputes between Moscow and Peking, they have a familiar way of evaporating where communism confronts the world of freedom." This is the very evaporation that took place between Belgium and the U.S.A. The latter had brought pressure to bear on the former to enforce their withdrawal from the Congo; but alas, their differences quickly evaporated into thin air. They joined hands, sang Auld Lang Syne, and marched right back into the Congo to repeat their history of massacres. It was Leon Damas of Guinea who said in his poem "Pigments,"

>"....my hatred thrived on the
>     margin of culture
> the margin of theories, the margin
>     of idle talk
> with which they stuffed me since

>            birth even
>    though all in me inspired to be
>            Negro
>    While they ransacked my Africa."

**Kerwyn Morris is a retired civil servant and was, for many years, Chief Fisheries Officer of St. Vincent. He presently lives in St. Vincent and the Grenadines.**

## MAN AND HIS RELIGION

By Marcia Harold

### Part I

(Taken from Flambeau, Number 2, September 1965)

Like all phenomena, Religion has evolved. It continues to evolve; to corroborate this one may note the new tolerance promoted by the Vatican Council and the new attitudes of most protestant sects. However, this article will not deal with present evolution and will barely touch upon past evolution; it has been written to illustrate man's grappling for the absolute through the medium of Religion. I say, through the medium of Religion, because in the modern world there is a growing attempt to seek the Absolute in non-religious, even atheistic philosophies, e.g., Jean-Paul Sartre and the Existentialist Philosophy and Ayn Rand and "Objectivism."

It is believed that all Religions developed from primitive Nature Worship probably because primeval man was overawed by the vastness and power of the Earth and its attendant phenomena (earthquakes, floods, eruptions, etc.) over which, moreover, they had no control. Primitive man conceived worship of the elements with the view to placating them. As his mind developed and he became able to grasp abstract concepts, the theory of morality originated, and the Gods now punished not only for lack of due worship, but the well-being of a community depended also on the maintaining of standards of morality. This led to the development of codes of law for living the Good life; this, of course, led to restricted morality and formed an integral part of Society.

The Hindu religion developed from Nature worship to which was added the consciousness of morality (what is right and what is wrong) and later, as man's mind graduated to metaphysics, they interpreted God as One. The Vedas says "Reality is One, sages call it by different names." But by the time this concept was reached, the Hindus had for centuries been pantheists and idolaters – the three-headed Shiva, the four-headed Brahma, Ganesha with the sixteen arms and Indra of the thousand eyes. There is divergence of acceptance of this concept; the masses give it a literal acceptance, but the intellectual interprets it as philosophic allegory

– the four heads of the Brahma, for instance, signify the breadth of the intellect of God.

To the Hindu, Brahman is One and everything is he, the material world and even man. They believed that man has deceived himself into seeing the world as complex. They believe that God is within the world, but also transcendent and more than the world. Brahman is indivisible, unchangeable, beyond Good and Bad action or inaction. Life is generated from within Brahman. So is the material world (Maya) which is still one with God but man is deceived into thinking that it has substance in itself; but this Maya is an offshoot of the real, but is not in itself the Real. Creation itself is a cycle and would be destroyed and renewed every 4,320,000,000 years in perpetuo. The material for the Maya is eternally existing and always was. Brahma creates, Vishnu sustains and Shiva destroys. Shiva destroys the form, but not the material.

The western mind has long linked practical morality to salvation, but the Hindu believes that one must be beyond both Good and Evil if one is to return to the heart of Brahman.

There is indeed a defined morality – Karma, the Law of the Deed – but this morality is really the specified duty of a caste and may differ among castes. These duties harmonized earthly society, but the Hindu concentrates on individual progress back to Brahman.

Hindu and western morality are conflicting; the westerner is preoccupied with the material world but the Hindu thinks this unrealistic since the world is an illusion and not permanent, and reunion with Brahman the only true reality which must be achieved to prevent endless reincarnation.

Buddhism was the rebellious offspring of Hinduism, and there are many basic differences, but the influence of the much older religion is apparent. Like the Hindus, Buddhists believe in Karma, the Law of the Deed, in reincarnation, and that the individual must work to release himself from re-entry. Also they have similar attitudes to renunciation of the flesh, to get above it – for example Hindu yoga, and in an extreme case, Zen Buddhism.

The precepts of this religion are based on the teachings of Prince Siddartha Gautama after he became the Buddha – the enlightened One. His doctrine taught that the world is ruled by Justice – from Good must come Good, and from Evil must come Evil; this is the first Law of Life. From this he concluded that prayer, sacrifice and supplication were of no avail, the Good life was everything. To do this, he expounded a code of ethics which the individual, and hence Society, must follow. Salvation (release) was to be sought and lay entirely within the individual. The secret of leading the Good life was to follow the Middle Way, extremes of either pleasure of asceticism being bad; his followers must advocate calm detachment. He taught the equality and brotherhood of man and rejected the Caste system of Hinduism. All peoples of the world could be converted to Buddhism, but Hinduism is only for born Hindus. Hence, in Hinduism, this concept of the privileged prevails in two ways: the degrees of privilege, caste by caste, within the religion and the Hindu as privileged against all others.

The end of the return to life to the Buddhist is to enter Nirvana (related to the Hindu state); it is the achieving of impersonal ultimate reality. There may be countless rebirths before this while the individual gradually purifies to enlightenment.

The Buddha never preached Divinity or worship but gradually his cult assumed all the trappings of a religion and became especially bastardized as it pursued its evangelical paths. The Buddha himself became a God, and statues of him reverenced. In many sects, the doctrine of salvation through faith has been added.

A Buddhist mythology has also developed which states that the Buddha lived on earth about 530 times in a variety of forms -- kings, thief, lion, etc., -- being known as Bodista in those lives before Enlightenment.

The Hinayana sect teaches that the individual pursues to gain Enlightenment for himself; but the Mahayana sect reverences the bodisattva who, on attaining Enlightenment refused to enter Nirvana but returned to assist others to this state. He is an intervener, but not in the manner of Mohammed or Christ.

In explaining the world, the Buddha stated it ever was, was not created and will never end, but Buddhists in their mythology have included a story of the Creation.

Confucian ethics was originally proposed as a guide for leading the civilized life within a well ordered society, yet this, too, developed into a religion. It is said that Confucius never pondered on the Divine at all. He seems to have been a sociologist concerned that the rulers must be just and the ruled satisfied.

The Ancient religion of the Chinese was based on ancestor worship, and this he encouraged because it helped to stabilize society by teaching respect for elders and tradition. He believed in the spread of knowledge as the answer to man's problems, and he believed in the power of love and in its infectiousness, i.e., if the rulers were good and just (which they would be through love of mankind) it will spread from class to class till it had infiltrated all society. It was because of his humanitarianism and his phenomenal wisdom that he eventually became deified in the minds of the people afterwards.

Chinese philosophers have been more concerned with life on earth rather than with contemplation of the afterlife. The Chinese by tradition have been earth-bound. The Hindu may believe that this world is of the real but not the real, but the Chinese have never doubted its reality, and sought to live not only in accord with existing nature but also with existing man. Their basic concept was that all existing elements (man, nature) were harmonized within a cosmic system, and therefore there should be a reciprocal relationship between both, if cosmic harmony were to be maintained. The unity between Heaven, Earth and Man was indivisible. They believe that the opposites of this world interact and are necessary to each other. Yang is the positive or masculine force; anything active, warm, hard, dry, bright, procreative, steadfast. Ying is the negative or feminine; anything passive, cold, soft, wet, dark, mysterious, secret, changeable, cloudy, dim and quiescent. In Chinese philosophy these opposites are in accord and if this harmony is preserved, everything good will abound.

Confucius taught that man's part in maintaining this harmony is to create a Society governed by justice and reverencing tradition. To Lao Tze, to produce from opposites, the order of nature, one must follow the Way (Tao).

Lao Tze left one little book, the Tao-Teh-King (The Book of Reason and Virtue), in which his philosophy is written. It says that he who wants to lead the Good Life must follow Tao; but he never really states what Tao is, which led from the beginning to much confusion. Is it Reason, the Word, God? However, in his lifetime he had taught retreat from civilization to nature in order to be in harmony with Tao; this obviously conflicted with the teachings of Confucius. His teachings, however, degenerated into a religion dominated by magic.

In China, one may be a member of all three at the same time, besides which they have all borrowed from one another. The Chinese had never speculated on heaven as a place for the life of the soul after death, until this was introduced to them as part of Buddhist thought, and Taoism developed 81 heavens as opposed to the 33 of Buddhism.

The Shinto religion of Japan is based on nature worship and worship of the Emperor, a descendent of the Sun goddess. It is pantheistic and has also added Buddhist belief and Confucian ethics.

The foregoing religions in one way or another had many deities, but the concept of one God is very old. There were two concepts of one God: a God of all the world and the God of one people (the Jews' earlier concept). The Jewish concept of a universal God developed as their history progressed.

## MAN AND HIS RELIGION

### Part II

(Taken from Flambeau, Number 3, January 1966)

The foregoing religions discussed in our last issue (Hinduism, Buddhism, Confucianism and Taoism) in one way or another had many deities, but the concept of one God is very old. There were two concepts of one God: a God of all the world, and the God of one people (the Jew's earlier concept). The Jewish concept of a universal God developed as their history progressed.

The Jewish and Christian concept of God is that He is One, omnipotent and the Creator of all that is: "And nothing that was made that was not made by him was not made."

Revelation of the omnipresent God came when the Jews realized that God was present with every Jew scattered in captivity.

When the Jews were captured by the Persians, they came into touch with Zoroastrian thought, but could not accept a creator divided in two; their God they said was Jehovah, creator of the world, the only Lord and ruler of the universe. It is supposed by some scholars that their present concept of heaven and hell was learnt from Zoroastrian teaching. A remarkable thing about the Jews, however, is that, captured and threatened throughout the centuries, they still retained their individualistic religion; nothing seems to divorce them from it, and it is one of the world's oldest religions; only the Hindu religion has also an origin lost in antiquity.

The Jews had always believed in the coming of a Messiah to save "My people Israel." It is believed that, because of the Persians, this idea matured into a savior of mankind; they still maintained however that he would be a descendant of David and would gather the Jews together into the Promised Land – a sort of preferential Jewish treatment. Judaism is not a personally founded religion.

Christianity grew out from Judaism, and it still retains basic Jewish concepts but to the Christian, Christ was, and is, the promised Messiah. To the Christian, Christ is Perfect Man and Perfect God.

Although one with God, he proceeded from Him to set the example of Perfect man and to preach the Kingdom of God.

Most Christians also believe in the Holy Trinity: God the Father, God the Son and God the Holy Ghost. The last proceeded from the Father and the Son, after the Son had been lifted up, to be the Comforter and Guiding Light of the world. Yet God is One, and God the Trinity is indivisible. Lead the Good Life and immortality will be the reward with God in Heaven; do otherwise and there would be the descent to Hell. The Judeo-Christian conception of reality after death is that it is not a state of loss of individuality into the heart of a Brahmam, but a real state of real life.

To the Christian, the approach to God the Father must be through God the Son; "if you have not known me, you have not known the Father." Christianity is the only religion in which God appeared on earth in the manner of Christ, and proclaimed the Son of God by Virgin Birth.

In the Islamic world, Mohamed is the prophet of God (Allah). Mohamed had studied the Bible and came to believe much of it and the Old Testament is contained in their religion. One day, Mohamed said Divine Revelation was made to him and he came to believe that he also was a prophet of One God and started his Life's work of preaching and teaching.

Moslems believe that God approaches Man through prophets, outstanding among them being Abraham, Moses and Jesus, but the greatest being Mohamed. The basis of the Moslem religion is Islam – submission to Allah; they believe in predestination, not free will. They also teach salvation through faith and worship of God, the reward for the Good Life being Heaven. Their idea of Heaven is a place where they will get all the pleasures they are accustomed to on earth.

All religions then teach a search for Truth and make attempts at defining reality. All existing societies have a history of religion behind them, their structures are the codes of law of their religions; no matter how secular the societies become, this, I think, would remain as the basis of their structure. Even so, man still ponders and will continue to ponder the truth of Divine Reality.

**Marcia Harold was a teacher in St. Vincent for a number of years. She presently resides in Barbados.**

## 21     OBSTACLES TO ECONOMIC GROWTH

### By Arnhim Eustace

(Taken from Flambeau, Number 6, November 1966)

Statisticians have verified the fact that two-thirds of the world's income go to one-sixth of the world's population, while at the other extreme, two-thirds of the world's population receive one-sixth of the world's income. The latter half of the statement refers to the worlds' so-called underdeveloped countries; the former to the developed areas of the world. We belong to the underdeveloped group. Why this discrepancy in the distribution of income on a global basis? It is because of the colonialist and imperialist tendencies of the now so-called affluent societies? Or is it that our people are lazy? Or perhaps we lack capital, or skilled labor or natural resources, or all three? Behind all these questions one thing is very evident, and that is, we have awakened from our lethargic slumber. This was not the gentle awakening that the legendary sleeping beauty had. It was something far more startling; we became aware, for the first time in centuries, of the now obvious discrepancy in the relative standards of living between the developed and underdeveloped worlds.

We are now wide awake. We want our standard of living to be on a par with the developed areas of the world. We want to derive the benefits of healthy economic growth. But such desires when stated are deceptively simple, for there are numerous obstacles to be overcome. And it is precisely with these obstacles that this paper is concerned.

The problems of economic development vary from region to region. But ultimately the development of any country depends on four basic elements: natural resources, population, capital, and knowledge or technology.

One of the main obstacles to the economic growth of an underdeveloped country is its political dependence on another more developed country. Indeed, the effect of political domination is that a kind of division of labor is established. But that is not the whole story; this division of labor is always advantageous to the dominant country. More and more, the dominant country specializes in the more lucrative pursuits, while the dominated country is generally limited to activities which yield poor returns, such as agriculture and extractive industries. Political dependence as an obstacle to growth in the underdeveloped countries of the world is not a matter to be treated lightly; it has to be tackled immediately and be defeated, if we are to grow. Planning for development while under domination is merely an illusion.

Besides political, there is economic dependence on a foreign power. This dependence on the part of the underdeveloped country can be detected in the nature of the foreign trade. Most underdeveloped countries are exporters of raw materials and importers of manufactured goods. Hence we are bound to be economically dependent on another country and have a low standard of living. Also, our countries are largely one-crop economies, or we produce very few products for home consumption.

The dependent country is thus powerless in the hands of the country to whom it sells the greater part of its exports. The price paid for these products are generally so low that our people are only able to receive subsistence wages, live in miserable conditions and are hard put to maintain normal working energy. International agreements on prices have done very little if anything at all for us because these prices are usually set by the big industrial powers who are usually the buyers of the very products for which they are setting the prices.

Some may argue that certain of our primary products do fetch high prices. But again, what good does that do us, since these are usually produced by foreign investors who export the profits to the dominant country. Such investments do not, and were not intended to contribute to our development. Since the profits are not kept in our country, a large part of our earnings from the export sector are used to meet the payments of profits earned by foreign capital. The extent to which this situation adversely affects the underdeveloped world and benefits the developed areas can be seen by looking at a particular case.

In its January issue (1958), the American magazine "Fortune" pointed out that apart from the export of goods and services from the territory of the U.S.A. which reached a figure of twenty thousand million dollars in 1957, there were in the same year 32 (thirty-two) thousand million dollars of American sales realized by the 2,500 subsidiaries of American firms established abroad. No comment is needed here except that I note the name of the magazine is most appropriate.

It is true that in certain cases foreign investments can encourage national investment and can be the starting point of some genuine development. But this is the exception rather than the rule. Such investments generally play a negative role. They encourage supplementary drainage of money earnings through the transfer of profits and even through the wages and salaries paid to foreign engineers and technicians employed by these companies.

Carrying their exploitation a little further, the companies formed by foreign capital, systematically limit themselves to the supply of the home market in many cases. This is to ensure that they do not compete with companies formed by the same capital, in other countries.

Thus far I have looked at two ponderous obstacles to the economic growth in underdeveloped countries. These are political and economic dependence on dominant nations. If our countries are to progress, these two obstacles have to be tackled at the outset by our leaders.

We have to rid our lands of exploiters. I am not against foreign investments per se. But when these investments play a negative role in the development of our countries they should be nationalized. The question then arises, is this going to be nationalization with or without compensation? This then becomes a function of the degree of drainage of funds inflicted on our economy in the past by the companies in question. It is also a function of the ideologies and temperament of our leaders. But first we must acquire our independence from the colonialist and imperialist powers. Without this independence, it would have been better if we had continued in our lethargic slumber previously alluded to.

For the purposes of this essay, I would like to divide the obstacles to growth into two groups. The first set with which I have dealt are external. I shall now look at what I call the internal obstacles.

Many economists consider lack of capital as the chief internal obstacle to economic growth. They maintain that this obstacle can only be overcome by appealing for foreign capital. Lack of key personnel animated with a real desire or capacity to develop the country is added to lack of capital in order to explain not only the present state of underdevelopment but also economic stagnation or slowness of present growth.

As a result of the low productivity of labor in underdeveloped countries, incomes are low, hence savings are very small. This meager amount of saving limits the volume of investments which in turn restricts incomes. Here we have what some economists call the "vicious circle." Low productivity – low income – little saving – small volume of investment – and back to low productivity.

The problem of our people is thus to increase capital – how is this to be done? Assuming that we have attained our political and economic independence, that is, we are now in a position to plan for healthy economic growth, shall we (bearing in mind the vicious circle argument) bring in foreign capital and thus bring back the very external obstacles which we had just expelled? Gunnar Myrdal in his brilliant book "Economic Theory and Underdeveloped Regions," strongly advocates the vicious circle argument. Professor Myrdal was the victim in 1958 of a vicious attack for his stand in regard to the vicious circle argument and his solution to this argument, that is, encouragement of foreign capital. The attacker was Charles Bettelheim, Director of Studies at the Institute des Hautes Etudes, Paris. He does not accept the inevitability of the "vicious circle," and hence the need to encourage foreign capital as the immediate solution. His idea is expressed briefly as follows: the most effective means of production is not necessarily the most costly. In other words, it is possible without additional expense to improve our labor productivity considerably – thus breaking the vicious circle. This paper does not permit me to go further with this view as it is concerned with the obstacles to growth and not their solutions. But suffice it to say that the Chinese have increased their agricultural production 4.5% per annum since 1953 by this method. Some countries resort to forced saving. This in itself may pose another obstacle, since it may mean that the people still will have no incentive to increase their productivity, for example, the Soviet Union is faced with this problem at the moment in its agricultural and industrial sectors.

Lack of key personnel has also contributed to our present underdeveloped state and it is one of the obstacles to growth. It is not surprising that we should suffer with this problem. In countries which were once politically dependent, or are still under the colonial yoke, most of the key personnel come from the dominant country. With regard to rapid training of political and administrative personnel, this obstacle is readily surmountable. Once we knock down the old social barriers that restrict the recruitment of key personnel to a strictly limited circle, we find that a great number of men emerge who are capable of taking the initiative and assuming responsibility.

I shall now proceed to spend a little time on population expansion as an obstacle to growth. Up to about 1800, the different countries of the world varied little in population structure. Heavy mortality combined with a high birth rate produced at best a moderate growth. But this does not hold good today. The developed countries through the improvement of medical facilities and certain methods of birth control (e.g., legal abortion in Japan have maintained a fairly moderate growth despite the fall in the death rate and the stability of the birth rate.

But the underdeveloped countries have been either late or reluctant or unable to follow the same procedure. While improved medical facilities and better sanitation methods have resulted in a fall in the death rate from approximately 45 per thousand to 15 per thousand, there has been, unlike the developed areas, an enormous increase in population. The reason for this is our reluctance to resort to birth control.

It has been estimated that it took the world approximately from 1 A.D. to 1750 A.D. to double its numbers. At our present pace this feat will be accomplished in 40 years. Also, if this pace is maintained, in 600 years it has been estimated that one square yard of land surface will be available per person. The phrase "standing room only" thus takes on an interesting, but ominous connotation.

High population density in some parts of Africa and the West Indies (Barbados) and in most developing areas readily suggest overpopulation. A readily expanding population has to support an increasing "demographic burden" which may absorb an excessive part of national production (both in consumer goods and human investment) to the point of making impossible the proper use of resources necessary to development. But despite this, no underdeveloped country has been able to effectively slow down its birth rate.

Japan has been most successful in doing just that. There, abortion has been legalized. This has brought a 50% reduction in the birth rate in ten short years. In 1955 there were 1,170,000 abortions compared with 1,727,000 live births. The encouragement of contraception by propaganda, and a wide-spread distribution of contraceptives had proved futile, hence the recourse to abortions. Bearing in mind the depth of religious feelings in the underdeveloped world, I cannot see them as willing or ready to accept such a proposal. Thus the population problem remains to threaten us. The danger is that such capital as is accumulated, may simply go into spreading a larger quantity of tools over a larger number of people without actually raising per capita productivity. This problem is likely to continue because death rates in our countries are still high relative to the economically advanced countries, and are likely to fall appreciably in the future. Furthermore, the increase in population is all the more serious in the underdeveloped countries where population is already dense in relation to land and other resources. In some extreme cases such as Java and Barbados, there are well over 1,000 persons per square mile. Under such circumstances, population pressure is not a stimulant to development as was the case in the U.S.A. but an obstacle or depressant. Because of lack of industrial capital, the growing labor force cannot find work in the city, hence adds itself to the already congested rural areas. Hence diminishing returns quickly take over. The number of workers on the land is already so great that the added labor brings no addition to production at all. The additional "hand" may seem to be working, but in fact they can be removed and the production will not be affected at all. This is called disguised unemployment and it is one of the symptoms of the deep population problems faced by our areas of the world.

Lack of facilities for education of the majority of our population is another serious obstacle to growth. It is education that moved us from our apathetic state, but much still is needed. Educating a people is not easy. It is possible to estimate the cost of constructing schools, etc. But what about teachers, without which the schools are useless? We can hardly find one-tenth of the teachers we need from among our own people due to the small size of the educated part of the population from whose ranks teachers are drawn. The issue is further complicated by the relatively large proportion of the people to be educated in underdeveloped countries. This is just one part of the story. There is the immediate need to reach the adults and provide them with the level of culture and technical education necessary to raise the economic level of our countries to the standards made possible by modern technology. That is why lack of education and educational facilities is an obstacle to growth. An educated and skilled labor force is of dire need to meet the requirements of modern technology and hence of industrialization leading to economic development.

Another obstacle to growth is our haste to adopt Western technology. Advanced Western technology, and in some cases Eastern technology, is by no means ideally suited to the conditions of the typical underdeveloped country. This technology has evolved along lines appropriate to the conditions of the country which created it. It utilizes relatively little labor and a great deal of capital, and depends on its operations on a reservoir of skilled labor and technically trained personnel. This is the exact contrast of the conditions in our parts of the world where labor is abundant or super-abundant, where capital is extremely scarce, and where there is an acute shortage of skilled labor and management.

Ideally the underdeveloped world would employ a technology which is neither the technology (Western) of a century ago (which is defective), nor the most Western technology (which is adapted to a different kind of economic context), but a third type of technology which consists of the adaptation of modern methods to the special conditions of the underdeveloped world. But this technology is a dream rather than a reality. Failing realization of this, the underdeveloped world has tried to import the latest western methods, with the consequence that it faces acute shortages in certain areas, capital and trained personnel, while it has idle surpluses, such as large numbers of unemployed unskilled workers.

Lack of natural resources may be an obstacle to growth, but fortunately "lack of natural resources" is not a feature of the underdeveloped world. But we are unable to develop these resources in many instances due to lack of capital, equipment and technical "know-how." but here again, foreign capital comes in and sucks the lifeblood of our country like the mythical "haig." I shall not go into this again, but it just reinforces a point I made earlier, that where foreign capital plays a negative role in our development, it must be stopped by whatever means possible.

Social factors have impeded economic growth in some regions. Social stratification based on land ownership has enabled the landlords to enjoy privileges at the expense of the peasants. This is an offshoot of colonialism and can be very easily detected in the West Indies. These landowners are not concerned with the economic development of the countries, but they have a vested interest in maintaining the present position. As long as they can continue their exploitation of the poor peasants and they themselves live in comparative luxury, just so long will they be opposed to any ideas that threaten their position.

Social and religious attitudes toward work have been an obstacle to growth in underdeveloped areas. The upper echelons of society look upon work as a sort of badge of inferiority. Hence much talent which might otherwise have been used to help promote economic development goes down the drain. The lower classes lack the incentive necessary for them to increase per capita output; and often they have a fatalistic attitude towards life (endorsed by religious philosophy) which does not permit them to think in terms of possible change. The refusal of a particular group to have anything to do with another religious group has also tended to be a hindrance to growth as in India.

This paper does not pretend to cover all or even half of the obstacles to economic growth. But I think I have touched on the main issues, and brought to light the fact that the task to be undertaken by us of the underdeveloped areas, is enormous. Firstly, wherever it still belabors us, we must free ourselves from the colonial yoke. The colonialists are not and were never interested in our development, unless it is of benefit to them. As the Prime Minister of Independent Trinidad and Tobago pointed out in his book "Capitalism and Slavery," "as soon as the British West Indies became negligible to British Capitalism, they were ready to free the slaves, but where other colonies in the east and on the mainland were still fruitful, 'the Mother Country' still retained the institution of slavery." In pointing out the "great interest" that the colonialists showed in the Congo, President Kwame Nkrumah pointed out in his book "I Speak of Freedom" that after 75 years of colonial rule, only one Congolese student had the benefit of a University education. Thus we must get our political independence.

Having attained this, we shall begin to reorganize our economies. We shall have to diversify our agriculture and industry in order to get rid of economic dependence. We shall then and only then be in a position to solve the numerous obstacles with which we are faced.

We of the underdeveloped world cover an immense area. We have the manpower and also contain strategic points controlling lines of communication. Raw materials such as petroleum, bauxite and iron are abundant; and what is more, the developed world are buyers of these raw materials, and we are buyers of manufactured goods. The two Power Blocs are aware of the advantages to be derived if they could gain our friendship. This explains the frenzy of aid and assistance being thrown at us. Fear is perhaps after all as efficient a motive force of economy as the lure of profit. Sordid self-interests mingled with displays of good intentions indicate to us, the underdeveloped nations, the road to follow. We know these outward displays to be a camouflage of necessity. We know it is to be a means to an end that is not ours. We are not going to refuse all aid, neither are we going to accept every proposal as a decisive fact. The days of meek acceptance of what "Mother England" or "Uncle Sam" or "The Iron Curtain" have had to say, are no more, because we are now awake.

**Arnhim Eustace was Prime Minister of St Vincent and the Grenadines from October 2000 to March 2001. He is presently Leader of the Opposition and President of the New Democratic Party (NDP).**

## 22         IDEOLOGICAL SANITY

By Cedric B. Harold

(Taken from Flambeau, Number 6, November 1966)

We live in a world of words which we create and which we claim to use as our tools. And yet, quite perplexingly, we often allow ourselves to be used by them. Having applied them epithetically to objects, we proceed to color them with whatever emotional ink happens to attach at the time to those objects, so that we react long afterwards in terms of accidental and past attitudes. This is most marked where very large numbers of people agree on the specific charge to be given to a particular word; and the effect is heightened where the same word carries a contrasting emotional significance to some other large number of people. The concepts which have the widest following, because they split the mass of humanity into fewer groupings, are racial and ideological. Racial epithets are no longer, if they ever were, descriptive, but connotative and divisive, and the same is true of ideological terms which are here our primary concern.

    The three major ideological labels are capitalist, socialist and communist, with the last two so closely connected that they are often confused. Communism is very much a bogey word; it is idealistic and cannot accurately be applied to any known state. The distinction drawn between Western states which practice socialism and their Eastern European counterparts is based on the degree to which the public sector in the national economy has supplanted the private sector, and not in any radical departure which warrants the use of the word communist. It will, for this reason, be ignored in the ensuing discussion.

    The proximate ground of ideologies is scarcity and insatiable greed – the classical economic problem. Its resolution is also largely economic, but at this juncture the boundaries of the intellectual disciplines cease to exist. The systems of production and distribution propounded impinge radically on social structure and organization and make demands on political, religious and other cultural aspects, all of which give to ideologies their packaged appearance. We see at the outset that they start from the same ecological conditions and have identical aspirations. Why is it then that capitalism is a dirty word in Russia and communism a dirty word in America? It is not proposed to answer this question here. There are many answers to it, depending on the approach one adopts; but the aim of this article is to encourage rational consideration on a local level of what ought to be the content - not the label - of a West Indian ideological model.

It has happened in St. Vincent that a politician has been asked to declare publicly whether he is a communist or not; Dr. Jagan in Guyana has come under the same fire; and in Jamaica only recently the PNP Opposition found itself having to deny that its label is communist. These questions are not asked to elicit information! All the relevant facts are known long in advance. Their force is condemnatory. For a man to declare himself an adherent of an alien ideology is tantamount to an admission of anti-national ideals and aspirations. The peculiar thing is this; insofar as these men are truly national, insofar as they have their entire being in the local situation, they cannot give a clear-cut answer to this question. What is demanded is a word that will hang him, but the only applicable words are neutral and emotionally meaningless. Indeed, there are no words but only a string of propositions which the accused in question is convinced will contribute to his people's welfare. It is uncanny how necessary it is to have a word for an object before one is allowed to judge it.

What is especially disquieting to the thoughtful citizen is the unfairness with which the inquisitions are conducted. A capitalist in the Western camp, is one who has faith in the proven virtues of capitalism, and who views its weaknesses as of small moment. To these same people a socialist is to be identified exclusively with the shortcomings of socialism, any good in the system being either ignored, or, at best, discounted. On the other hand, the socialist claim that their influence has modified capitalism into producing better working and living conditions for all, is only partially true; both capitalism and socialism operate under a banner of growing humanitarianism, which is the true provenance of so-called socialist legislation.

The font of social ills in theoretical capitalism is to be found in the superordinate place in which capital and the ownership of it are held. Not the liberty of the individual but the freedom of the owners of capital is fundamental to the system, and it produces the sort of inequalities which make some men to be the serfs of others. Feudalism was capitalism when land was the major productive resource; it became transformed and had its name changed after capital as a separate factor came into prominence. The economic base was altered and a new propertied class arose; what remained the same was the social division into those with special privileges having power over those without.

The socialist thesis is that this discrepancy can be overcome by state ownership of the means of production so that power is abstracted from any caste group and placed, so the saying goes, into the hands of everybody. Actually, all that it has achieved so far is the creation of a new basis of privilege predicated on ideological orthodoxy. In Russia, the desire to take power out of the hands of interest groups has resulted in the concentration of all power into the hands of a monolithic institution which is judge, jury and executioner – hardly the most human answer to the inhumane use of power. The Russian and Chinese systems are totalitarian in their institutions, but their vaunted socialism is purely mythological.

The sanctity of capital is, as had been said above, the distinguishing feature of capitalism. Socialism, bred out of disillusionment with capitalism, attempts to restore the preordinance of the brotherhood of man. It fails, and every historical precedent points to its continued failure, because men have never lived in brotherly unity – at least, not the variety that dreamers often imagine. Men have always been dishearteningly individualistic, and will continue, despite the best designs of socioeconomic planners, to be this way. This is why socialism in practice has to be so doctrinaire and hence, so unrealistic. The sanctity of capital has been supplanted by the sanctity of a formal set of ideas, and its owners are the only ones entitled to hold sway in the socialist order. What is needed in the West Indies, and indeed throughout the world, is an ideology which is not doctrinaire, which relates always to human meditation and is capable of evolutionary development. Words and institutions have an unhappy manner of getting out of hand. In actual fact, it is not they that change; men and the times change, but the institutions are eternal. As Veblen remarked: "institutions are set up to meet pre-existing conditions, but their very presence alters the situation they were designed to correct, calling for ever newer responses. Societies fail when they elicit no new responses".

The above should suffice to show how far removed practical realities are from theoretical lucubrations. The question to be asked of any social reformer is not which label he wears but how appropriate are his proposals. Once we can develop an open mind on major issues and weigh statements on rational grounds it would be possible for any individual to put forward proposals without risking charges of treason or heresy. This would mean that any given proposition will not be thrown out because it smacks of an alien label but considered in the light of existing configurations and modified or discarded only if they are either irrelevant or too drastic. Drastic reforms are to be abhorred because they disturb equilibria faster than accommodations to the new levels can be made.

It is worthwhile to know the point of divergence between the American and British flirtations with capitalism. America is a vast country and in the hey-day of pure or free-enterprise capitalism, there was no hindrance to a man pulling up his roots when he was not satisfied and going elsewhere. Capitalism flourished, but sensitive souls were not straight-jacketed into serfdom. Land was free to those who had a pioneering spirit, so that nonconformity carried no hard penalty, nor was there any pressure on the capitalist order to humanize its prescriptions.

The position was different in Britain where population had outstripped its available resources. The immediate effect of unbridled capitalistic growth was widespread and unmitigated human suffering. The new order enforced conformity, and, being inadequate to the needs of all, anxiety and privation were endemic. Hence the early growth in Britain of humanitarian movements and what has later been identified with socialist ideology. It was not any racial genius or brilliance that helped the British to overcome these conditions; it was the extent and duration of dissatisfactions which even those at the helm could no longer stomach, and which those below were not any longer prepared to endure.

Their different situations have resulted in a far-reaching body of social welfare legislation in Britain; while in the U.S.A. we have witnessed a fantastic ideological battle over the Tennessee Valley Authority (TVA) proposals, and more recently over President Johnson's Medicare Bill. The contribution of TVA is now unquestioned, but it was opposed purely on the ground that it was inconsistent with the capitalist ideology. No doubt the same sort of unrealism was evident when the Russians decided to introduce the profit motif into Soviet industries. The significance of this to the West Indies is the lesson it teaches in terms of the relation between realism and ideologisms; where the realities speak out, ideology must be silenced and be made to accept even that which is inconsistent with it. This being the case, it is nonsensical to oppose reforms which appear to be taken from a contrasting ideology. At times and on an individual level, opposition is symptomatic of intellectual pride – the ability of someone to recognize that such and such a proposal is of socialist or of capitalist provenance; and, given whichever political situation prevails, all he needs to do is to exaggerate his charges and multiply them in the certainty of arousing some emotional reaction.

The promise of socialism to the West Indian mind is a new world in which dependence on the owners of capital and land is a thing of the past, in which class interests are replaced by something more fundamentally human; and where the art of government and politics is not any more how to rule, but how to maintain and develop a framework within which people with essentially human interests can live. The practice of socialism across the Atlantic has not anywhere lived up to expectations. What is especially debilitating is that the great socialist introspections, their analyses and recommendations for reform, are not available for our study; so that while we learn the theory of, or as is more commonly the case, the propagandist catch-phrases, we are blissfully unaware of the pitfalls and what has been tried to correct them. The danger, then, is that our pursuit of the above aspirations can easily be turned away into the blind alleys of socialist dogma merely because of a dependence on the word socialism. Hope for the future must therefore be, not the pursuit of socialism, but of those things to which our people aspire. Identity of ends does not guarantee identity of means, and in this case, we are not even knowledgeable as to the means.

Our society awaits the codification and designation by a name of these aspirations as a preliminary to reaching out for them. There are many examples before us; the Egyptians have preferred to retain the word socialism; K. Nkrumah invented "conscientism," while the original American scholar Eric Fromm has offered "communitarian socialism," partly to distinguish it from totalitarian or bureaucratic socialism. Finally there are documented accounts of attempts to live a life which resembles what we are after, dating from the Cooperative exercises of $19^{th}$ century France and England, through the experiments by Alfred Noyes and others in U.S.A., to further French and Italian attempts still in progress. They have largely been a history of failures, but out of them can come new knowledge which could surely prove beneficial.

**Cedric Harold is a computer scientist at the University of the West Indies. He is presently living in Jamaica.**

## 23 THE SCHOOL AND THE COMMUNITY

By Claudon Fraser

(Taken from Flambeau, Number 6, November 1966)

In many instances we come face to face with the task to decide what the word "community" means. Almost invariably we tend to associate one or more groups of workers as "Community helpers," while we accept the efforts of the rest as a mere matter of course. For example, the policeman is often looked upon as the monster who sets out to paint the label of crime on others; the Public Health Inspector as the stumbling block in the butchers' road to financial bliss, as well as the active machine of a supposed repressive Housing Authority. Needless to say, the teacher's only function is to create Einsteins out of every child who is committed to his charge; and, especially in the rural districts, the good qualities of a teacher are determined only by the number of examinations which his pupils may or may not pass.

With a bit more careful thought, we can, according to my way of thinking, be able to see the various workers in the social field as well as those in the technical and scientific, forming one large body, resembling somewhat the worker bees in a hive.

Everyone is acquainted with the term "school;' it conveys to the mind any institution where knowledge is obtained regardless of how small or great the amount may be. The Community is the human environment, the people among whom the influence of the school spreads. It is the human climate in which the school operates, a citizenry that is not a loose gathering of atomized individuals, but a group of people who are knitted and welded together by some social cohesive bond. However, it must not be believed that there is an invisible hand which coordinates the efforts of the various individuals, so that if each does his bit without thought of the others, there would be this spontaneous coordination and cohesion. It is from this point of view that I want to outline the means whereby the school may so operate in collaboration with other organizations in order to fit itself for the performance of a positive role in the community.

The three aspects of school life, according to A.G. Hughes are (i) the curriculum, (ii) extracurricular or out-of-school activities and (iii) human relations. Looking back at earlier civilizations, or even at the patterns followed by earlier societies of Western European civilization, we observe quite readily that more often than not these three aspects were never outlined in their educational policies. The Jewish boy was "brought up at the foot" of one of the Rabbis where he learnt the law and the prophets. In ancient Greece the Spartan was trained for the army, while the Athenian became versed in the classics. Much closer to our own time, we learn of Medieval England with the various Craft Guilds in which her youngsters were trained to build or to weave as the case might be. We see, therefore, that in some way or other the needs of the community were being met out of the general plan of training. In fact the community's needs really dictated the particular educational policy.

The various changes in the political, economic and social spheres of life have brought with them new problems which never existed in earlier generations; and it is to these new problems coupled with those already existing that we have to address our thoughts if we must satisfy all these aspects of school life.

Man is a gregarious animal, that is, he must form himself into groups, and in many instances we find him benefiting from his linking himself with his fellows. But though he may have some interests and aspirations common to those of his fellows, he certainly possesses others which are different from theirs and in fact peculiar to him as an individual. Therefore, if these natural tendencies are to remain untended, chaos must result and reign in the community; and, to avoid this, efforts must be made to reconcile the wishes of the individual with those of his fellows. In other words, a true community spirit must be developed. "The good community," says one writer, "is a democratic community in which everyone is free to participate freely, and on terms of equal status in projects of joint concern to him and his associates."

In any socially healthy community, the school acts as the hub around which every other thing spins, and it is therefore requisite that the image of the school and its teachers be properly projected to the searching eyes of the community. The teacher must set a good example to the general public by his conduct, appearance and deportment. In fact, his general attitude must reflect his profession and his community. This responsibility does not rest with the teacher alone; much rests with those responsible for the administration of the school, as the part played by them can promote or not promote the proper image of the teacher in the community. A teacher who is not respected by his employers has a very slim chance of winning the respect of his community. In many instances teachers are sent to work in remote areas without the slightest bit of convenience provided for them; consequently, they are forced to lead substandard existence. Poor housing, lack of almost all domestic facilities, all tend to bring them down below the social level of his more fortunate counterparts in other avenues of state employment. As a result, the public esteem for teachers is relatively low, and there is little appreciation of their community activities whether in or out of the school. If, on the other hand, the teacher is made free from all grouse, he enjoys that sense of security and so gives of his best. There is a freer atmosphere in which he can join with other community workers in creating a well ordered, harmonious society.

In developing such a community, the school must play a major role. Not only must children be taught the technicalities of language and mathematics, but the social sciences must be so well presented as to bring out the humanistic side of them. In some countries of the world, there are special schools charged with the task of Community Development, for example there are the Community Schools in the Philippines, the Basic Schools in India apart from what can be termed Traditional Schools. Perhaps much can be said in favor of those special schools in the countries mentioned, due to their social set-up; but I venture to state that the job can be accomplished by our schools with only a few minor modifications. In order to create the "good community," the school should be so organized as to give adequate freedom to the pupils; but the teacher must bear in mind that neither children nor adults can really enjoy freedom until they have learnt to accept the responsibilities of freedom. However, the more likely they are to develop and maintain a free and satisfying community life when they grow up.

It may be argued that enough is being done in our schools to that end. Moreover, there are numerous textbooks about the development of character, leadership, citizenship etc. in our school libraries. But textbooks in themselves can only assist people to pass examinations, while we learn to live from example and actual experience. If the teacher merely puts the facts to his class, he is depriving the youngsters of that privilege to learn to live. He must make every effort to relate the new experience, where possible, to those in the pupils' environment, and should point out where one affects the other. In other words, he must so make his lesson live that they serve the desired end; that is, creating worthy citizens.

However, in many instances the teacher finds that his plans for community development are frustrated because he does not receive the cooperation of all concerned, including parents; and this may lead him to withdraw himself from the subject completely. If, on the other hand, the effort is organized on a larger scale, the teacher may ally himself with other community development workers in order that grown-ups and children can be introduced simultaneously to the new ideas. Therefore in

organizing community work in the schools there are three major points which must be borne in mind:
(i) the teacher cannot effectively educate the children for community life if his purposes and those of the community conflict; rather, the successful education of the children depends on the successful education of their parents together with the rest of the adult community.
(ii) the teacher cannot effectively educate either children or adults if he is held primarily responsible for educating both.
(iii) although he should be relieved of the major responsibility for educating adults, he can nevertheless give other community education workers very useful help.

These points provide a sound and practicable basis for working out a policy which neither sacrifices the educational interest of the children nor arouses the antagonism of their parents, nor hopelessly overloads the teacher. And being freed from the primary responsibility for the community education of adults, the teacher is free to think of the children first and to choose the curriculum and teaching methods which meet their needs best.

One important fact that needs special mention is that no amount of force brought to bear on the teacher or any other community worker can produce the desired result. The worker must first be convinced that what he is expected to do is worthwhile and purposeful; and the first means of achieving this prerequisite is proper training. Secondly, authority must be decentralized as far as possible as, for example, allowing a reasonably free hand in designing syllabi to suit the particular needs of this community. Thirdly – and this comes as a corollary to the second – the emphasis on examinations should be suitably modified.

Consequently, the Training Colleges must be so geared as to (a) train the teacher in what to teach and how to teach it; (b) show him how to develop initiative, leadership, and socially responsible attitudes among children and (c) give him some kind of experience of community work among adults. Moreover, the more teachers-in-training are given responsibility in college societies and activities generally, without more than remote control from the staff, the better will they be able to understand the principles of self-help and cooperative efforts for the community.

After all the necessary prerequisites have been obtained, there remains the last hurdle to surmount – people are naturally aversive to change; and the idea that the school can act as an important agent in community development is not readily accepted. This is because many educational administrators, teachers, and others believe that the proposed new purposes for the school will adversely affect its existing work, and they sometimes doubt whether the school can effectively undertake them. It is therefore essential that in the construction of the curriculum, a proper balance be observed so as to satisfy the needs of the learner, not only for easy adjustment to his community, but also for his intelligent participation in national and international affairs.

To sum up, permit me to state that the ultimate objective of education for community development is not only a balanced and integrated personality but a wholesome and harmonious society. In the development of such a society, the school becomes an instrument of social and economic change, and the teachers and bigger pupils play a large and effective part in programs of social and economic welfare.

**Claudon Fraser was an elementary school teacher. He died in a tragic plane crash off the coast of St Vincent and the Grenadines in 1977.**

## 24 REFLECTIONS ON RACE RELATIONS IN THE UNITED STATES

By Jean Norris

(Taken from Flambeau, Number 6, November 1966)

[EDITOR'S NOTE: The following article was written for Flambeau by Miss Jean Norris, a teacher of English and Journalism at North Carolina College, Durham, North Carolina, U.S.A. She spent five weeks in St. Vincent in June and July 1966 in connection with work for the Baha'i World Faith. The article reflects some of her observations and her views on certain social changes in America.]

When one reflects on evolving race relations in the United States over the last few years, one sees a panorama of conflicts and their resolution, of revolutionary changes tearing away the fibers of well established traditions, of racial bitterness, and of a growing respect for individuals on the basis of talents and skills. As a special article on the Negro revolution in an issue of Newsweek magazine stated in 1963, no revolution is tidy. The same publication noted that the term "revolution" is rather loosely used when referring to the current social struggles in America, for the Negro is not striving to overthrow an existing regime but rather to become integrated into the national mainstream from which he largely has been excluded, and the means of getting into that mainstream are many and sometimes at variance in method.

Explosive changes in human affairs historically have been marked by conflicts in personalities, methods and purposes; but when studied in perspective, the various occurrences have led, nearly always, to the opening of new vistas in human relations, to the birth of new awarenesses and to the death of stagnant traditions. Such has been the case in the accelerated changes in America that have affected every aspect of the national life, from the legal through the educational, political, economic, literary, social, and all other facets of living and creating.

Not unlike the breaking of the shackles of colonialism on various islands and in Asia, Africa, and South America, the conflicts in the United States are deeply rooted and variegated. Rooted, as in the West Indies, in years of suppression under a system of slavery, generally the Negro had outwardly accepted, through the first half of the twentieth century, the pattern of segregation that grew after the period of Reconstruction, but the growing inner resentment and bitterness were like a smoldering fire kindled gradually by his observations of an increasingly booming society in which his role was less than vital, and sparked within the last twenty years by his identification with the dark peoples of Asia and Africa in their assertion for independent rule.

For years before the 1954 U.S. Supreme Court decision on school desegregation, the legal staff of the National Association for the Advancement of Colored People and the Urban League had persistently worked to improve the lot of the Negro, as in the integration of various state colleges, and in work in slum areas. But in spite of the efforts of these organizations and the journalistic outburst in the Negro press against injustices, the Negroes of the nation remained largely immobilized as a social force. It was not until the 1954 Supreme Court ruling that the schools of the nation should be integrated "with all deliberate speed" that a far-reaching impetus came, and not until the 1957 Montgomery, Alabama bus boycott that a unifying force emerged. As a few Negro parents sent their children into formerly all white schools to test the strength of the new law and to open doors for the masses of Negro children, the colored people of the nation and others dedicated to justice became allied in sympathy with the audacious elementary and high school students in this their pioneering experience. The walls of hate and intimidation were met with extraordinary determination to destroy barriers of segregation and the double standard of education. The belief in the rightness and long term value of their actions led the Negro parents and their children to endure economic reprisals, threats, bombings and other pressures exerted by those who opposed an integrated educational system.

As moves to implement the 1954 Supreme Court decision increased, various subsidiary effects resulted. One such effect was the heightened activity of the Ku Klux Klan, largely composed of whites of low economic status, and the formation of Citizens Councils, primarily composed of white businessmen and others of the middle class, dedicated as the Klan to interference with the movement towards integration. Physical and psychological pressures and articles in the press were used in the attempts to halt "racial mixing."

Another effect of the pressures surrounding the court decision was the migration of hundreds of Negroes to Northern cities where they sought relief from a treadmill of problems, only to find other frustrations in the slums of the North. So it was that the large Negro population in the South became more mobile, adding to the great World War II migration settlements of Negroes from the South to the highly industrialized states of California in the West, Chicago, in the Midwest, New York in the East and various points between.

In times of tension, more people are forced into taking stands for or against vital issues. Thus, another effect of the extended period of the integration of schools was that fewer people were apathetic, as various political and civic leaders, newspaper editors and others were put more in a position of having to take a stand. Various forums, editorials, and countless conversations of average citizens focused on the issue.

The second far-reaching motivation cited that led to the recent rise of civil rights activities was the Montgomery bus boycott. Beginning with a single tired and quietly determined woman – Mrs. Rosa Parks – who was arrested when she refused to move to the back of a city bus, the Negro population of Montgomery, Alabama, became unprecedented in its unity as thousands walked and formed car pools rather than ride the segregated buses. Not only did a spirit of unity of effort and a confidence in the rewards of the boycott method emerge, but also a leader, Dr. Martin Luther King, Jr., who was to become the unifier of the various classes of Negroes in Montgomery and eventually to become the national symbol of the Negro's fight for the full gamut of civil rights.

So it was that the token integration of Negro schools, as highlighted by the early Little Rock, Arkansas and Clinton, Tennessee episodes, and the early mechanism of the boycott, as highlighted in Montgomery, Alabama, paved the way for what may be called the "sit-in stage." The scattered school integration confrontations gave the promise that the whole pattern of racial separation in the South was on the brink of a sharp change, giving to the civil rights picture a scope in area and a depth in significance. The Montgomery boycott contributed an understanding of solidarity of purpose and effort through an organization among the Negroes themselves, allied with others sympathetic to their cause. Through the bus boycott in its triumphant conclusion, the Negroes saw that it was possible to change oppressive patterns themselves by exerting effort rather than waiting solely for the change of laws through the court process to help implement justice.

Thus, when a group of Negro youth sat at an "all-white" lunch counter and requested service in Greensboro, North Carolina on February 1, 1960, the stage had been set for widespread efforts, both spontaneous and organized. One week later, students at North Carolina College at Durham had initiated efforts, returning to the campus to relate stories of rebuffs and insults that motivated others to join the sit-in efforts. Fights sometimes flared, breaking the passive resistance pledge as demonstrators faced slaps, pin-prickings, and food thrown upon them. But, as a whole, the youth held true to their pledge to endure humiliations with stoic determination free from violence, a technique that was to draw sympathy and to put the federal government fully behind their efforts. So the sit-ins went throughout the South, with sympathetic demonstrations from one coast of America to the other, as numerous whites joined the movement. And as the sit-in grew in numbers from the big cities to the small towns, so grew the mass jailings that accompanied them and concurrently the organized method. Pronouncedly, the civil rights groups began focusing on action techniques as their meetings came to include demonstrations and practice sessions in sit-in tactics and in self protection. Human relations councils were organized or strengthened during the period. And the civil rights spirit came to permeate the Negro college campuses as "We Shall Overcome" became the theme and motivation.

From the sit-in technique, combined with the boycott in stages of the movement, came the integration of lunch counters in ten-cents stores through much of the South. By 1963, another move of demonstrations came as the civil rights groups increased the scope of their attention to restaurants, movies, and job opportunities. The picket line, which had become widely used after the initial sit-ins, was used again along with other pressures for negotiation. Fair employment practices and provisions for patrons were the emphases. From this wave of the movement came the opening of certain jobs and of certain recreational facilities.

Continuing to build in momentum and in the number of participants, the civil rights movement was highlighted by an unprecedented march in August 1963, the celebrated march on Washington. This demonstration attracted thousands of persons from over the nation, from the humblest of workers to the wealthiest of movie stars, representing various racial and religious backgrounds and national origins – all allied in the desire to take a stand in the movement that had snowballed from that first impetus of the Montgomery spirit. This quiet and dignified mass demonstration during the time the U.S. Congress was debating the Civil Rights Bill, contributed strength to the argument for its passage. Upon its institution into law came the opening of public facilities of the nation and broader employment opportunities from the cities to the small towns. Although many businessmen protested the passage of the bill, once it became law, doors were opened throughout the South. In some places the law was obeyed begrudgingly as Negro patrons were overcharged or given less than satisfactory service, but to a remarkable degree, businessmen accepted the ruling as the law of the land. So it is that many of the same restaurants and theaters that were once scenes of intense racial conflict are now quietly integrated as though they were never otherwise. This is not to say that all facilities have been tried, for in some of the very small towns there are likely places yet untested because of various pressures from the whites or a certain apathy among the Negro citizenry, but by and large, public facilities have been integrated throughout the South.

The employment aspect of the Civil Rights Bill has also brought far-reaching effect as industry increasingly searches the Negro college campuses for their most capable graduates. The growing demand for talents and skills is illustrated by the fact that seven years ago fewer than ten industrial representatives visited the North Carolina College campus in quest of its qualified graduates, whereas now more than two hundred representatives visit the campus and offer remarkable starting salaries and benefits to those who meet the standards of employment. The current dilemma in some circles is that there is a greater demand for qualified persons than there are persons qualified. Negroes, long denied entrance into certain areas of employment, have sometimes been hesitant to train for these fields although their services are now in great demand. Others have broken into varied fields and are now serving on all levels of employment. The Office of Economic Opportunities on the federal level has done much to check into cases where bias has been charged and to open new areas.

As the Civil Rights Law received its first testings throughout the South, a new phase of the rights movement emerged, that for voting rights. Coming from this chapter, and accompanied again by demonstrations, was the Voting Rights Bill that provided for federal registrars to register Negro voters in places where they were denied this right. As a result of this new stake of Negroes in the political picture where their numbers are many, numerous ones are running for local, county, state and national offices and numerous white politicians are now appealing for their votes. One indication of this new political strength is in Georgia, a state whose history has been marked by evidences of the most rabid racial hatred and strict segregation. Here there are now several Negroes seated in the legislature, as there are in Texas and other states. As illustrated by the most recent mass march, the one to Jackson, Mississippi, the push for large scale voting among Negroes to effect more long range and widespread changes is the current focus of the rights movement, as housing and other areas receive subsidiary attention.

With Dr. Martin Luther King Jr.'s recent move to Chicago to accentuate racial injustices there, the South no longer was the single focus in civil rights activity. Restrictions on apartments, houses, and areas where Negroes may live have long been frustrations. Even more than in much of the South, the North and Far West are marked by bias in housing, for unlike the South where integrated neighborhoods are not uncommon, the North and the Far West are characterized by large scale slums and restricted areas. Because of the density of population and degradation of conditions, these areas are veritable powder kegs that have erupted into such incidents as the Harlem riots in New York City and the Watts riots in Los Angeles, California. The Poverty Program of President Lyndon Johnson's administration has provided some help in these areas but, as whole, limitations in local administration and problems of method in the still relatively new program have left much to be desired in giving real relief from existing conditions. Moreover, the program has worked on living conditions and training of school dropouts through the Job Corps, not in desegregating areas. An open occupancy bill currently being debated in the U.S. Congress would provide much relief from pressures, but many people see little chance of its passage, recalling the recent defeat of such a bill in the comparatively liberal state of California and considering the biases of many Northern and Southern Congressmen on the issue.

Beyond the areas of housing, employment, public facilities, and education are others where legal aspects are being debated. Two major ones currently in focus are the jury system which has excluded Negroes in many parts of the South, and the laws forbidding interracial marriage which remain on the books in some states. Following several widely publicized cases of the miscarriage of justice stemming from civil rights incidents, President Johnson has proposed legislation to deal with inequities in the administration of the jury system. The means of implementing such changes are yet to be set forth. The second additional area of current civil rights concern cited, inter-racial marriage, is now before the U.S. Supreme Court in the case of an inter-racial couple whose marriage is considered illegal in their home state of Virginia. If the Supreme Court decrees that such laws against marriage on the basis of race are illegal, the most touchy area of civil rights will be reached, for it is the matter of racial mixing on this level that has been most frightening to those against integration. The statement that one may marry whom he chooses in essence recognizes the unity of race, the human race, which the segregationist has always denied.

So it has been that, through the combination of the quiet procedure of the courts and the more vocal process of the demonstrations and their allied activities, the climate of America has undergone, and is undergoing, phenomenal changes. Those changes have reached into all areas. In the armed forces and in sports, through those primary areas since 1954 cited in this article – education, public facilities, employment, and political rights – integration has become extended into more and more of the professional, civic and social organizations; in press coverage and into representation in advertising in the mass media, and on such levels as the beauty pageants.

Additionally, the Negro's role in the theater is a new one reflecting his new image. The flat stereotyped character of a shuffling, docile and complacent Negro of earlier plays and films has been replaced by a many-faced character, reflecting the various levels of action and response that are evident in all human behavior. More is yet to be done in realistic representation, as in representing inter-racial love affairs, but as a whole, the movement is in the direction from the stereotyped to the individual portrayal. In acting itself, recognition is being extended as indicated by Sidney Poitier's being chosen the outstanding actor in the film world and Bill Cosby's being selected the outstanding actor in the television field in recent annual competitions.

In conclusion, in viewing the changes now occurring in the United States, I see them as a Negro, as an American, and as a Baha'i. As a Negro, I see them as belated and still only partial relief from the humiliations and injustices that Negroes have suffered from the time of their enslavement. I feel firmly a need for a personal and spiritual amity to make the new integration something more than a cold legal evidence.

I see the changes as an American as the gradual fulfillment of the constitution of the United States which extols basic human dignity and upholds the rights of the individual. In the Negro's current pressures for full recognition then, he, as some have phrased it, is helping America rediscover its conscience.

As a Baha'i, I see the struggles as inseparable from the great changes that are going on throughout the world, for Baha'u'llah, the founder of the Baha'i World Faith, prophesied in the nineteenth century, an incomparable period when long held traditions would be swept away, a time when mankind would gradually recognize the unity of the human race, in time the unity of nationals under a world federal government and the basic unity of religions under one God. He prophesied that America, an incomparable melting pot of the various races, nationalities, classes, and religions would be the microcosm through which would be reflected a future world unity, a fulfillment of the Christ-prophesied Kingdom of God on Earth. It is in this direction in belief, effort, and dedication that I see the panorama of changes in America as bursting with unprecedented promise.

**Jean Norris was an ardent member of the Baha'i faith in America.**

## 25     C.L.R. JAMES – THE MAN AND HIS WORKS

Report Delivered to the Conference on West Indian Affairs

University of Montreal, October 9, 1965

By Martin Glaberman

(Taken from Flambeau, Number 6, November 1966)

    I first saw C.L.R. James in 1938 when he came to the United States on a lecture tour. I saw him keep the rapt attention of an audience of several hundred people in New York City as he lectured for three hours on the British Empire. I last saw James about a year and a half ago at his flat in London. We had several days of intense discussion of the Negro question in the United States. My wife and I had just returned from a trip to continental Europe and one of the most delightful evenings I have ever spent in my life was spent listening to James discuss the long list of statues and other works of art that the traveler in Europe is supposed to see. He brought to life Michelangelo and the days of the Medici in Florence. And not only brought them to life, but made them most relevant to our own day.

    Between these two occasions, I have seen James lecture in New York and to an audience of auto workers in Detroit and keep them equally enthralled. But what I associate most in my own mind with C.L.R. is not so much his ability to give to others of his own store of knowledge and wisdom but rather his ability to draw out of others knowledge of themselves and to develop the talents and abilities that are in them. In his writings, in his lectures, in his conversations with individuals, the outstanding characteristic is the development of the reader or the listener.

    There are people in many parts of the world who are familiar with the work of C.L.R. James. Apart from the West Indies, there are share-croppers in Southeast Missouri in the United States whom James worked to organize in the 1940s. This was 20 years before Martin Luther King and the Student Non-violent Coordinating Committee began their work in the South. There are South Africans who secretly used "The Black Jacobins" as an underground textbook in the struggle for freedom. There are cricket lovers in England who found their experience of that spot deepened and enriched by the writing of C.L.R. James whose experience of modern industrial society was recorded and their understanding made more profound by C.L.R. James. There are in many countries thinkers, writers, teachers and politicians whose education and training came in part from James personally and from his works.

Yet, despite all this, the significance of James and of his work is little known and hardly understood. In part, this is because much of James' work is unpublished and out of print. But more important than this is the tremendous range of his interest and his accomplishments. Many people have seen the trees which he has planted, but few have seen the forest.

James has written a novel, a play which was produced in London and a number of short stories. He has written a history of the rise and fall of the Communist International. He was the first to write of the case for West Indian independence. His "The Black Jacobins", the story of the first successful slave revolt, was written in the cause of African independence. He was one of that small band in England, the African Bureau, who fought and educated for the freedom of Africa when, to most men, it was only a dream. George Padmore was the head of the African Bureau. James was the editor of its papers. Jomo Kenyatta was a member, Kwame Nhrumah became a member.

But his interest and his talents were universal, not to be limited by a nation, a continent or a race. His translation of Souvarine's biography of Stalin and his studies of the Soviet Union and of economics led to the development of a theoretical point of view which made possible a serious understanding and critique of the Russian dictatorship, a point of view which is fully in the revolutionary socialist tradition and retains for that tradition its democratic essence. His study of, and writings on, modern industrial society have illuminated the social process for many who would otherwise have been lost in the confusion so characteristic of those who think about the problems of the modern world. And his work is characterized, not by the dullness of the scholar's ivory tower, but by the fire of the participant; and not by the supposed impartiality of the academic, not by the pessimism of the small in heart and mind, but by the optimism of one who can see the broad historical process and can see, above all, the life, the talents, the contribution to freedom and to history of the millions of ordinary people who inhabit our planet.

James wrote a study of Melville, the American author, which provided a unique interpretation both of Melville and his works and of modern American society. This book, "Mariners, Renegades and Castaways", is now one of the standard texts of Melville's criticism. He has used his knowledge of Shakespeare to illuminate the modern political personality and to rekindle interest in Shakespeare himself, in broadcasts for the B.B.C. and an unpublished manuscript on Shakespeare and Lenin. In "Beyond a Boundary", through his understanding of cricket, he has helped both West Indians and Englishmen better to understand themselves and their cultures. It has been called by English reviewers the finest book on sports ever written.

In his writings on, and participation in, the struggles of Negro Americans, James has put forward conceptions of that struggle which cut away narrow ideological and group interests and place the Negro American at the center of the historical stage in the United States, the most revolutionary of Americans.

It is easy to believe that this tremendous range of work and thought reflects an individual genius who has simply exercised his talents in many fields. That would be only a half-truth and therefore wrong. For the many and various questions which have occupied James during most of this century are not separate and unrelated but are parts of a unified totality. The unity comes from a fundamental philosophical point of view which can be described as dialectical. It is that the world is torn by contradictions, that the contradictions are the struggles between men, and that men knowingly or unknowingly, make their own history; and that the fundamental thread that runs through and illuminates the history of mankind is the continuing struggle of the great masses of ordinary people for liberty.

We want to mention two books. One, unpublished, is called "Notes on the Dielectic". It was written in 1948 as an effort to apply Hegelian and Marxian dialectic to the understanding of our own time. It is both philosophical and concrete, and so perspective was this philosophical tool that, eight years before the Hungarian Revolution, James was able to indicate, in abstract and theoretical form, what the Hungarians demonstrated in life; that is, that the domination over the masses of the industrial countries of the traditional political party had come to an end and men would, for the first time, take their fate directly into their own hands.

The second book is called "Modern Politics". It was the result of the six lectures delivered at the Public Library in Port-of-Spain, Trinidad. It was published as a book in Trinidad, and immediately suppressed so that only two or three copies are now in the possession of the author and his friends. The book presents the panoramic history of the western world in a way that is understandable to anyone. It shows the struggle for human freedom continuing in all ages and on all continents. And it offers to the reader the means to understand his own history and, what is more important, means to make his own history. It is small wonder that the book was suppressed – but it will be republished.

It should be clear that it is my view that C.L.R. James is a world figure of the greatest importance. He is, in a very real sense, a citizen of the world. But he is, because of that, very much a West Indian. It is not an accident that such a man was born in Trinidad. It is part of the contribution of the West Indies to the modern world. The West Indies has what is essentially a European Culture. And this is embodied in C.L.R. James to a degree that would be difficult to match. But unlike Europe, the West Indian intellectual has not experienced the unparalleled catastrophes and defeats that have been the fate of Europe in this century. Two world wars, the defeat of revolutions in the major countries of Europe, the barbarism of Nazism and fascism and Stalinist totalitarianism, all this has made of the European intellectual a cynic and a pessimist. As a result, to many Europeans, the narrow view has seemed more rewarding than the broad view.

In C.L.R. James is embodied both the totality of Western culture and the optimism and fire of a people who have not been defeated by history, who have still to make their own history. He is not the least that the West Indies has contributed to the world.

**Martin Glaberman was a worker in the auto industry in Detroit for twenty years. Later he returned to academics and was Professor of Social Sciences at Wayne State University, Detroit, Michigan. He died in 2001.**

# 26 FACING REALITIES IN POLITICS AND IN ECONOMICS

By: Cedric B. Harold

(Taken from Flambeau, Number 7, March 1967)

Arnhim Eustace in "Obstacles to Economic Growth" (Flambeau, November 1966) expressed certain convictions which are both provocative and disappointing. Provocative because they challenge the prevailing dispensations, and disappointing because, unsupported by objective references, they remain mere opinions. This is particularly evident in his treatment of foreign investment about which he writes: they "generally play a negative role." He defines clearly enough what he means by negative role, but by omitting to lay any factual basis for the statement, one must need abide by one's previous information which, in this instance, is to the contrary.

This is not intended as a critique of the November essay. It is, if anything, a partial critique of the first sixteen paragraphs, but I would prefer to consider this the second salvo in a debate just begun. I have gone outside of Mr. Eustace's own terms of reference with its focus on obstacles to a re-evaluation of some other widely held views.

## POLITICAL DEPENDENCE

There is not much to say about the relation between our colonial system and economic development. We have always been sugar plantations to the Imperial Interests, and progress had only two dimensions – abundant sugar supplies and a convenient market for British exports. To achieve the one, they constructed the plantation system with or without slavery; and for the other, nothing positive, but the negative tariff structures and the Navigation Laws. To have made the market grow (as in U.S. colonial policy) would have meant an emphasis on local development to which their attitude was characteristically negative. So they restricted their strategy to removing their competitors (mostly Dutch) to the detriment of all West Indians.

Although political independence is a desirable goal, one must beware of overstating its connection with economic growth. The former does not contain within it the seeds of the latter. We stagnated, not because we were not politically free, but because the nature of our political bondage contained obstacles to growth. Remove it and you remove an obstacle – it is an essentially negative act. Political independence, if it means responsible government, will provide a new soil and a new stimulus resulting in higher growth levels – but only if it means responsible government.

It is, I think, important to emphasize this point. Political independence does not mean responsible government. All it does mean is that legislative formalities will be concluded in Government house, St. Vincent, instead of in Whitehall, London. In the case of the major powers, independence has meanings other than the ceremonial: it means that the decisions reached in their capitals reflect local initiative, aspirations and capabilities more than they reflect reactions to external considerations. With small countries, however – with Jamaica, Trinidad, Barbados, Guyana – local decisions of international import are largely responses and accommodations. All over the world parliaments, congresses and assemblies follow a similar procedural pattern: politicians gather, talk and pass laws – but not all political decisions are as important as others.

Apart from the content of independence, there is the question of executive responsibility. This is partly a function of the constitutional articles, but largely it is a function of the caliber and devotion to duty of elected politicians. We in St. Vincent have had politicians who have mastered the art of politics – men whose astuteness and political canniness make them the equals of the best anywhere in the world – but men, by and large, so engrossed with the performance of their art that they seldom pay attention to government. Given the choice between playing sterile colonial-inspired roles and politicking, our candidates, to the extent that they were skillful politicians, chose the latter every time.

There are two lessons here: one is that it lays bare the lie that the colonial tactic was geared to giving our people experience in the practice of government. What we got instead was the development of politics to a high art and a colonial heritage of non-responsible government. The second lesson refers to the future and questions whether both the system and the present crop of politicians are fitted for responsible government in independence. Can they forget political rituals sufficiently to make any system work in a way that will benefit the country and ensure democratic (as opposed to oligarchic) ideals?

In as much as colonial government was a poor example to learn from, and since our politicians chose not to learn anyway, our society faces the challenging task of having to build and learn at the same time. There will always be the danger that the worse aspects of the colonial heritage will be remembered as the easier alternative to constructive endeavors. As a buffer against politicians, therefore, the society is going to have to rely principally upon its civic minded citizens and its trained and devoted civil servants. Indeed the civil service is pivotal during the next few years to the whole future of St. Vincent. And we are going to need the service of an unbiased daily press.

## ECONOMIC DEPENDENCE

"Dependence," Mr. Eustace writes, "can be detected in the nature of our foreign trade." This is, of course, true. What is also true, however, is that "the nature of the foreign trade" is what, among other things, defines dependence and independence. If our foreign trade were to resemble that of Britain or the U.S.A., such an alteration would not lead to, but rather would reflect, independence.

Part of the difficulty here is the stigma which the word "dependence" carries. At the moment, it signifies that which must not be. The current ideology dictates that we be absolutely independent in every possible way – politically, economically, culturally. There are some who declare we should dress differently and talk differently, without, unfortunately, ever saying what we should actually do. Economic independence is therefore regarded as a goal in the same way as political independence with the exception that its meaning is largely negative. Precisely, it means not being economically dependent.

Haziness about goals and vague assumptions about our capacity to achieve them mean that wishful thinking has pride of place in national planning. It becomes easy in the circumstances to build our whole future upon dogma ("We have to rid our land of exploiters," "investments that play a negative role should be nationalized.") and declare such things as costs and social organization irrelevant. Hard facts are the nightmares of many reformers, but they must be faced, and they include dollars and traditional social processes. They include the acknowledgement, furthermore, that whether we like it or not, our economy is backward and is dependent. Practical politics for us does mean accommodating ourselves to a framework defined by the highly industrialized countries, and this in turn imposes a logical limit to the targets that are within our reach.

We can put this in another way by saying that our status is dependent because of the gap between the standard of living we try to maintain and that which we can maintain through our unaided efforts. We can only maintain the existing level of living by importing commodities produced in the industrialized countries, and in order to buy them we must earn the foreign exchange. This on a practical level means trading what we have on available markets. Immediately it means exporting bananas, arrowroot, copra, provisions, etc. And not only exporting these things, but accepting the price which the purchasers are prepared to pay.

Having stated the hard facts, we can turn our attention to the range within which we can maneuver. Here we find that what we trade is a function of what we produce, and that the price obtainable can be influenced by ourselves under certain conditions. We produce those things which our productive resources enable us to produce and from which we can derive the maximum income yield. Certain commodities yield high returns on the international market – airplanes, tractors, nuclear generators; certain others do not – sugar, bananas, arrowroot. We do not produce the items in the first set (however much we may wish to) because we do not have the productive capacity to do it; we produce those in the second set because, of the things which we can produce, these yield the highest returns. At the same time we need many of the items in the first set. It is our here-and-now capacity, our actualized potential, which in the last resort defines our dependence, and it must be emphasized that capacity is not a function of wishing, nor is successful technique a function of dogma.

The art of maneuvering within the range is the art of government – an art which, one hopes, will attract the attention of the politicians we elect to office. Successfully practiced, it results in growth trends in the economy and enables us to say that we have good government. Conversely, lack of growth is a measure of poor government. The targets in successful international maneuvering include the following: attracting foreign capital on the best terms available; obtaining technical and financial assistance from the U.N. and other media which provide them; entering into or initiating international associations which would further our interests; negotiating trade pacts which are favorable to us. Locally it would include fiscal and monetary policies as well as direct government participation in the field of production. This is the government function in its economic aspects.

## FOREIGN INVESTMENT

Foreign investment has always been a thorny subject. We both need it and mistrust it. Castro's historic expropriations merely exemplify the extreme consequences which mistrust can bring.

Foreign investors are not today the exploiters they once were because they operate within a framework of internationally accepted regulations. When an independent country accepts foreign investment, it might not be as favorable as one would like, but good government is surety that it was the best obtainable. It is not a matter of take it or leave it, but rather of how to take it, since have it we must.

Mr. Eustace's mistrust of foreign capital enabled him to discern investments with negative roles, and for which he has a ready remedy. "But when" he writes, "these investments play a negative role in the development of our country, they should be nationalized." The difficulty with this statement is that the condition is not a normal one, otherwise there is every reason to terminate the exploitation. Foreign investments are welcomed – are sought, in fact – because they are expected to, and invariably do, make a positive contribution to economic development; it is all a matter of the terms under which it comes . Poor government, or government by self-seekers whose indicators of progress are rates of flow into their pocket may – and do – negotiate harmful contracts, but this is not something a good government and alert citizenry cannot change.

As for nationalization as a policy, what need be said? Socialist preachment of nationalization is premised on social and not economic foundations; it is designed, not to increase production or even to maintain it, but to reduce disparities in wealth. If the British Labor Party succeeds in nationalizing steel, its consequence will not be any increase in production or productivity, but the reallocation of claims to income at present enjoyed by a small circle. It has, however, been seized upon by many, including non-socialists, who attribute to it certain magical properties of economic healing but which, on final analysis, only reflects either ideological bankruptcy or animosity directed towards present wealth-owners.

The idea of nationalization without compensation deserves out-of-hand condemnation. It is unfair. Responsibility for any investment contract, unfavorable to the borrower country, rests exclusively on the government which permitted it, and either they pay the penalty or no one. The duty of a succeeding better government would be to renegotiate the contract and not off-hand to expropriate, and certainly not to expropriate without due compensation.

One point needs to be hastily made: exacting a penalty from members of an erring government has meant, in certain parts of the world, persecution to the point of execution. Not only is this barbarous, but it fails to recognize that a people always – everywhere, every time – get precisely the sort of government they deserve. If irregularities in the discharge of political responsibility are suspected, then commissions of inquiry should be set up to investigate such charges. And if they are proven true, then the guilty person should be tried under existing Civil Law and not under any Political Code, however constituted.

**Cedric Harold is a computer scientist with the University of the West Indies. He presently lives in Jamaica.**

## 27 A TEACHER'S LIFE AND TERMS

### BY MARCIA HAROLD

(Taken from Flambeau, Number 7, March 1967)

This article is designed to be a reflection of the everyday life of a teacher in a secondary school; a glimpse of school environment, classroom activity and a philosophy that governs a teacher's thoughts and actions. Any teacher ought to recognize the hurly-burly of her world; the philosophy may, however, be only in part hers as it is in the main self-derived and hence there may be disagreement with some of the methods and attitudes underlined that are governed by this philosophy.

The years a teacher spends teaching are the years the teacher gets taught. From the moment she enters her first classroom she begins to learn the do's and don'ts of living with the live material occupying chair and desk, and of giving life to what could so easily become dead data, which is fatal. Those are the two mind teasers of the beginner and they remain her foremost concern to the end. Life is a long course of gaining experience that leads to self-confidence, which generates ease of manner and an ability to recognize what quality is needed to really make a moment live.

There are, however, many more burrs that cling to her skirt complicating her life; old ones reclinging and new ones blown by the wind of artful hands and artless faces. These include limited space, the common cold, staying indoors as much as possible during Guy Fawkes, and irritable parents.

In our schools, a chronic enemy is overcrowding. In some cases there is hardly space between child and child, and child and teacher. If the day is hot and humidity high she teaches through the blast of hot air that in addition assails her from their bodies. Usually in our schools this is not the condition in all form rooms for the classes are usually whittled down in number the higher the grade. But picture the teacher in the furnace of the Lower school and sing a song of those saints.

The myth of the teacher relaxing during morning and evening breaks persists. Without doubt, one sometimes manages to relax (usually in the form of lively debates with the staff) but this is by no means regular. Many of these breaks are taken up in settling quarrels among the pupils, dispensing punishment, correcting exercise books, having a look through the lesson to be next taught, getting the advice of other teachers, and answering questions posed by students. Not to mention that every teacher has known days when she spends an entire break working in a classroom for one reason or another only to hurry out in time so as not to be late for the next class assignment. The same is true for so-called off periods.

During each term the teacher must act as judge and jury, and the truth is not always easily arrived at so that decisions can be made, for the teacher likes *just* decisions, not just decisions. To whom does the pen (book, etc.) really belong? Whose fault was the fight? Is the child feigning illness? Is that excuse a lie?

One of the occupational hazards of the teacher is parting a fight between two lusty combatants. She commits this folly at her own risk, for she is liable to be belted one in the eye before the sense of sanity once more descends. Another occupational hazard is to come before bribery: "Teacher, I'll bring six eggs for you tomorrow if you let me off," while the tears come coursing down the pupil's tormented cheeks.

What else is the teacher? Nurse. Grazes, cuts, headaches, period pains, fainting, a sudden rash from allergy, must all be given first aid accompanied by kind words, sympathetic looks and reassuring smiles. A teacher is truly a chameleon, changing color to suit each role at a moment's notice, and roles so different from each other.

Each day also brings the role of counselor. One may be employed to teach history, but in the course of each Term one is asked literally to help solve the riddle of the world. It is not that a teacher ever gives the impression that she knows everything, but simply that the minds of growing people, becoming more aware of the world and seething with ideas, pose these questions to you not as one who necessarily knows but as one whose opinions they respect and who can at least reason with them The teacher has a vantage point of more experience, and this the students know to take advantage of.

The teacher is mentor but she is friend and it takes such patience and sagacity to strike the balance that results in the pupils' giving the teacher due respect without her creating a barrier of aloofness.

The pupil must feel confidence in the teacher. Not only the confidence that she knows the subject she is discoursing on but the confidence which leads to voice a barrage of questions and to be able to confide their worries about their work. This means painstakingly listening to every question hesitantly posed by the bravest during the first term of getting to know each other. The others soon get courage. It means not giving scathing remarks at silly questions or answers or, much worse, the cruel laugh.

When one knows the temper of a form, and one is an old friend of weeks' standing, one may relax the above rules somewhat. Why? Because friends are not formal with each other and the give and take of class life is good training for the outside world.

No teacher learns all the above from the word "go," but learns as she goes along and makes many mistakes. In spite of good fellowship the teacher remains very much in charge. This is necessary so that you have the authority that must be obeyed for instance to bring a class back from involved argument to the continuance of the subject in hand. This authority is usually so understood that it is obeyed without the actual use of it. At times, of course, even the best behaved form needs to be pulled up.

The teacher, too, loses her temper at times, but this is usually from constant provocation (it could be aided by a headache and the weather) and venture a spate of rhetoric against an individual or a class, but these full-blooded outbursts are not often and are said in language so much above their heads that they lose half of it. They have a lesson in themselves, for when it is finished it is finished and one launches in an ordinary voice into the lesson and the children are aware they can ask any question without getting "barked." Because of the confidence and trust they are aware that no malice is held against them, and this is important.

What is this governing philosophy? Never add salt to the rumor of infallibility. When a subject for debate comes before the form directly, from the subject being studied or out of the blue, the attitude is "Come let us reason together" instead of the teacher propounding her view and that being that. She throws forward her ideas as her opinion, they consider it and offer theirs – not necessarily in that order – and in the end may even agree to differ if they have not been completely overwhelmed by the teacher's logic; but all are happy that they have participated in a battle of wits and opinion on equal terms. The idea is that although every effort must be made to complete syllabi that are not the only thing that is important. It is equally important that they acquire the capacity to reason, that they develop character, and have some idea of even the most controversial topics of this world so that they do not walk through the school gates like innocents abroad. While learning the facts in the set books the attitude should be given that here we have in our hands not a book with facts to imbibe but a book of ideas whose relevance we must search and question for. Thus one imports not only knowledge but a love of knowledge, reason and logic that must never cease to grow.

In the midst of it humor must not be an outcast. It is an invaluable asset, a sense of humor. A teacher delivering a joke from the rostrum has its place but is unbeatable in informal combat where you laugh at others and learn to laugh at yourself.

One thing that a teacher must accept and be understanding about is that individuality is diversity. A form will be comprised of mischievous ones, born talkers and natural practical jokers. Trying to break them with unyielding firmness is fatal; you lose and the child is made stubborn and abjectly rude, and the ruinous vicious circle is created. One must also consider, however, that many children are brought to school already the worse for mishandling. Channel their energies, join sometimes in their illicit humor, give them a chance, then you take your chance. If you can't beat them join them, and they will soon realize that they can't beat you and join you. The result is a happy class because of the room for personality development instead of repression.

In the teacher's life and terms much has not been mentioned here, such as the giving up of holidays to help the students and the numerous piles of books that must be taken home to be corrected. But with all the side irritations it is a job in which one gets supremely involved and fulfilled.

**Marcia Harold was a teacher in St. Vincent for a number of years. She presently resides in Barbados.**

# BEYOND A BOUNDARY: A REVIEW

### By Timothy Hector

(Taken from Flambeau, Number 7, March 1967)

"Beyond a Boundary" by C.L.R. James is not an autobiography; though about cricket; it is not a cricket book; though prominently featuring the masters of cricket, its purpose is not biography. Its story is cricket and cricketers within and beyond a boundary.

The book forms the second part of a trilogy in which C.L.R. James attempts (and succeeds) to unveil and bring to light the essence of Western Civilization. The first part of the trilogy is *Mariners, Renegades and Castaways,* a study of the American Classic *Moby Dick,* and so a study of twentieth century America. There is nothing in literary criticism quite like it.

Beyond a Boundary is a view of British Civilization and the West Indian relation and contribution to that civilization. In the book Caliban and Prospero have met and not only speak the same language, but common to them is a means of artistic expression, Cricket. Mr. James' thesis is that cricket by its very nature is not only an art but has within it the sustaining qualities of a human ethic – an ethos all the more necessary in the extreme world situation of our disjointed times.

Such an immense assignment could easily lead to the prolix in style, and the diffuse in method, but Mr. James being quite familiar with the novelist's craft employs that economy of narrative which is art, together with a penetrating simplicity of style which keeps the book aimed at the ordinary reader.

The result is a magnificent story, arrestingly told, and signifying the eternal effort of man to rise above the dehumanizing process, be it of colonial oppression or industrial oppressiveness and, in rising, find expression for his many and varied endowments.

With such a perspective brought to cricket, W.G.Grace, C.B. Fry, Constantine, Headley, and his Mastership Gary Sobers illumine the history of our times, and their achievements though personal (and rightly so) must therefore be seen as a contribution at the rendezvous of human history. Mr. James in a succinct and masterly analysis traces the growth of organized games and popular democracy and shows that the fuller the sporting life of man, the wider the degree of popular democracy. It is an entirely new historical perspective, ranging from the Greeks in their unequalled democracy to Caliban's sojourn in the New World and the latter's struggle for popular expression in art and politics.

The remarkable freshness of the book lies not only in that it says what has never been said before, but in the author's method. That method Hegel formulated when he stated that truth lies in plotting the precise distance between the observer and the observed. Hence the autobiographical details which are limited to James' relation to cricket, and which career has as one of its summits of interest the author's tremendous campaign for Alexander to go in favor of Worrell. West Indian cricket has not been the same since.

In fact so much that has highlighted the cricketing world is within the covers of this book, the Wizardry of Pigott behind the stumps, the furious pace of George John, the overwhelming elegance and tragic failure of another West Indian great batsman Wilton St. Hill, the ruthless execution of bowlers by Bradman, the power of Walcott, the craft of a Ranjitsinjii, the grace and power of a W.G. Grace and the W.I. Board's complete misunderstanding of Gilchrist. All of this is recounted not as cricket reminiscence, but much of this provides the author with the basic material for his brilliant argument with the famous aesthetician Bernard Berenson. This chapter, "What is Art" does not answer Tolstoy's agonizing question, but it widens and deepens the discussion by including games as a medium through which man expresses himself in motion and in craft.

I still have some reservation as to whether cricket with its 'confusion of actuality' can or should be placed alongside the plastic arts. I prefer to place it among the 'lively arts' – the dance, the opera, the movies, etc. That apart, there is no reason for disagreement with Mr. James' view "that it is an unspeakable impertinence to arrogate the term 'fine art' to one small section of man's quest for the perfect flow of motion."

A comprehensive review of "Beyond a Boundary" is virtually impossible, for it is self=contained and self-explanatory. Its importance does not stop at the statement that it is the finest book written on a sport (as some have claimed) but in the far more significant fact that in the voluminous literature of our times nine out of ten books have as their fundamental tenet that gloom and dread, anxiety and anguish, comprised the essential ingredients of the human mind. These books by talented writers are the whimper of a dying civilization. "Beyond a Boundary" is a direct and forthright challenge to that conception of human life and establishes C.L.R. James among those of 'Undying Vision' who see the possibility and constituents of a truly human history.

"Beyond a Boundary" is part of Caliban's contribution against the threatening world catastrophe. When the third part of the trilogy, a study of King Lear, is completed this body of work will stand in its own rights as the most impressive intellectual contribution of the West Indies to the cause of universal emancipation. It is enough to remember that the Black Jacobins was written in 1938 in the cause of African freedom. In 1938 the African struggle for freedom seemed remote. It now is foremost in the modern world. James' view of the movement and inexorable development of a world society may well come to pass.

What do they know who only cricket know? "Beyond a Boundary" answers the question fully.

**Timothy Hector was the founder-leader of the African-Caribbean Liberation Movement (ACLM) based in Antigua and publisher of the Outlet newspaper. He died in 2002.**

# SLAVERY:
## TOTAL INSTITUTION OR TOTAL SYSTEM

By Castine I. Quashie

(Taken from Flambeau, Number 8, September 1967)

Now that we are at the crossroads of history I believe that it is essential for us to make an assessment of our existing social situation by attempting to place St. Vincent's present position in some kind of defensible perspective. Most people tend to take the status quo as given, as their starting point. The result has been an incomplete grasp of the processes and forces at work in our social system and a correspondingly distorted view of the system itself. I have chosen slavery as a convenient launching pad in my effort to throw some light on the forces that have shaped our social personality and fashioned our social structure. I will first of all outline two parallels with which slavery can be compared – the total institution and the total system – and I will draw my own conclusions. As the treatise unfolds the reader will, I hope, appreciate the propriety of the treatment chosen.

According to Goddman, in his book - Asylums - "Total Institutions are organized groups with well defined boundaries and a marked hierarchical structure, for example, inmates and staff in Asylums, prisoners and warders, officers and men on a ship at sea, slaves and masters. There is a fundamental division between "staff" and "inmates," the former being free to move outside the institution and to have some measure of contact with other groups in the wider world, whereas the inmates live out all aspects of their lives in the institution. Whole blocks of people are treated as units and are marched through a set regimentation under the surveillance of the small supervisory staff. Staff tend to feel superior and righteous while inmates are conditioned to feel inferior and weak. Passage of talk and information between the two strata and between inmates is restricted and inmates are deliberately kept in ignorance of what is to happen to them, this being part of the mechanism of establishing and maintaining control. The structure of relations in a total institution is calculated to rob work of any moral significance.

It is a crucial characteristic of total institutions that people enter as socially formed personalities with a culture and a set of attitudes which need to be replaced so that the inmate can be 'handled." Mechanisms are brought into play designed to destroy the inmate's old self so that a new set of attitudes, a new 'identity' can be imposed. The treatment involved induces a "state of anxiety, insecurity and humiliation which leads to the inmate's ready acceptance of his new role as a relief from the anxiety itself."

Elaboration of two examples of the total institution will serve the present purpose. The first is the Asylum. An individual is committed to an Asylum when his physical and emotional ability to face the strains and stresses of everyday life have broken down and are suspect. He goes to the Asylum in something of "unconscious willingness." In a sense he is glad to be in the 'Asylum, "away from it all." There he makes an adjustment to the absolute authority of the institution. He is told what to do and when to do it. An obvious behavioral characteristic is a reversion to childhood, to a pattern of behavior that is puerile to the outside observer and from which initiative and responsibility are absent. The second is the Monastery. There is no doubt that an individual enters a monastery of his own volition, some from an earnest conviction that this is their calling, others to get away 'from the evils and pressures of this world.' There he goes through the process of mortification – the very word is significant and apt – designed to sweep away his former personality in preparation for the new. He is made to leave all his clothes and former possessions behind. His name is changed. He is given a new identity. He is subjected to a harsh discipline with an unusual emphasis on authority and obedience to his superiors and a higher power. Personal initiative is discouraged. All activity is directed from above. He makes a complete adjustment to absolute authority.

A classic example of the total system is the concentration camp. Students of Psychology will forever be indebted to those courageous souls who scribbled in the half light and recorded their physical and psychological experiences in the Nazi concentration camps. What will be said here about the concentration camp as a total system is drawn from a book entitled "Slavery" by S.M. Elkins, who has drawn upon the experiences of the survivors of Nazi concentration camps.

In the 1930s the Nazis devised a system of concentration camps as an instrument of terror. Later the value of the camps was recognized in the Nazi scheme of things not only as an instrument of terror, but also of control and became a permanent feature of the Nazi operations. Incoming prisoners were deliberately tortured and subjected to all kinds of physical and psychological stresses in order to break their resistance and pave the way for their degradation and humiliation, the psychological purpose of which was to destroy the old personalities and create malleable creatures upon which new personalities could be forced. Brutalities were not merely permitted or encouraged, but prescribed. In order to survive the new inmate had to make a rapid adjustment in terms of personality and behavior to absolute power in the concentration camp, an adjustment which in fact meant a new personality, a new creature with different habits and behavior, a stranger to his former self.

In the first instance, in response to the extremity of the initial tortures, the new prisoner experienced what is known as psychic detachment, a "splitting of personality," a "real" feeling that the experiences were not happening to him as a subject (person) but as an object (thing). This sense of detachment had a double function: it was an immediate psychic defense mechanism against shock and it was the starting point toward a new adjustment.

Secondly, "Be inconspicuous" was the formula for survival. Those who indulged in bravado or heroics were quickly eliminated. Initiative was a dangerous quality and it was of value to live in selfish isolation. One might befriend an individual who led one into serious trouble and death. Those inmates who made the successful adjustment necessary to survive assumed a child-like quality in behavior. Sexuality disappeared from their talk and there was an abnormal preoccupation with excretory functions. They lost many of the customary inhibitions as to soiling their beds and their persons. Their conversation was trivial, their sense of humor silly with giggling abundant and apparently pointless. Dishonesty and lying were chronic.

Thirdly, there was a more or less intensive identification with the S.S. guards, the source of all their misery and degradation, but also the spring of whatever privilege they enjoyed. "The prisoners firmly believed that the rules set down by the Gestapo were desirable standards of human behavior, at least in the camp situation." They imitated the S.S. guards in drill, posture and brutality, often being more cruel to their fellow inmates than the S.S.

As evidence of the system's effectiveness three points may be cited: (i) the inmates cooperated with the guards to the extent of digging their own graves; (ii) there was no hint to revenge when the possibility presented itself upon liberation – the inmates had come to accept completely the superiority of their Nazi masters; (iii) the relative scarcity of suicides in the camps. "The simplicity of the urge to survive made suicide, a complex matter of personal initiative and decision, out of the question."

But despite all the cruelties and brutalities there were still clear standards of paternal benevolence, no matter how narrow the sphere, stemming from the fact that the Nazis were human beings dealing with human beings. In the aftermath of the liberation it was found that the majority of the previous "campers" were unable to make a constructive adjustment to freedom and a free society, but those who had were those who had been given a meaningful task in the camps and allowed to exercise a meager measure of initiative, that is, those whose work had had some measure of positive moral significance.

There are obvious points of similarity between the "models" of the total institution and the total system. For the present purposes stress will be laid on two points. In both cases there is (i) an initially induced state of anxiety and humiliation designed to erase the former personality and make way for another (a new "identity"); and (ii) the emphasis on regimentation, absolute obedience and the suppression of initiative. But it might have been noticed that it was stated that the total institution involves an adjustment to absolute *authority*, whereas the total system involves an adjustment to absolute *power*. This was meant to emphasize an important difference and indicate a preference. The "model" of total institution fails to stress the element of brute force which comes out so strongly in the total system. Individuals are forced into total systems. Thus for purposes of comparison with slavery the parallel of the total system is chosen, in particular the "model" of the concentration camp.

The points of similarity between (the processes involved in the adjustment to absolute power in) the concentration camp and under a system of slavery are manifest. It will be enough to outline them in brief for they are sufficiently close to produce much irritating repetition. Nor is there any desire to get too emotional or hysterical about the discussion. Emotion and hysteria always tend to generate more heat than light.

First, there is the process of degradation and the psychological response of "psychic detachment." The African was rudely captured from his familiar native village and brought by force to a strange environment. His dignity as a human personality was dragged in the dust. The process began on the march from the village to the slave station on the African coast, where the unfortunate "creature" was handled and tested for strength in much the same way as one treats an animal in the market place. It was continued on the long voyage from Africa to the West Indies – the notorious Middle Passage – during which the slaves were shut up for most of the time in the stinking holds much as any inanimate cargo. At the sight of the slave ships entering the harbors West Indian planters would rush down excitedly to handle and fondle the slaves. Little wonder that the slaves looked dazed and glassy-eyed. Some of them, puzzled and confused, jumped into the sea in panic and drowned themselves. At the ports the planters made their selection and the survivors of the Middle

Passage were handed over to the highest bidders. Next, they were taken to the plantations of their owners and subjected to the last part of this phase, the process of 'seasoning,' designed to break the African for plantation life. The process of degradation of personality was complete. It was certain that those who had survived the Middle Passage and 'seasoning' were on the path of adjustment to their new situation and stood a good chance of survival.

It is apparent that in a social system based upon force those spirits that refuse to be broken and shaped by the whip and torture represent threat and are a constant source of anxiety and fear. Either they must be 'tamed' or eliminated. Under a regimented system of forced labor initiative, leadership and creative energy were inevitably stifled or at best seriously curtailed. The plantation Negro found that it was to his advantage to live up to the image that had been drawn of him as a child savage that needed first to be civilized and then led. To be able to dissemble and lie "truthfully" were useful arts in the battle for survival. Fawning adulation and selfishness were important parts of the paraphernalia of success. This was the process which produced the Sambo, that familiar stereotype of the Negro as a child-like talkative creature tripping over his feet to please his white superiors. He was good fun and entertainment, especially when it came to song and dance; his sense of rhythm was superb. Though reasonably useful in matters of little weight, he was immature and incapable of shouldering responsibility. He was a liar and a cheat, but nonetheless a likeable fellow.

Finally, the Negro Slave was convinced of the superiority of his white masters. For all its harshness the system had its human side and definite standards of benevolent despotism. The slave was assured of certain privileges so long as he was not intractable and his behavior indicated a belief in the superiority of his white masters and his own inferiority. Hence the crucial importance of the Sambo-type behavior. There was an intense identification with whiteness and white values as the most desirable standards of behavior and a fierce neurotic rejection of black and colored and all their associations. This identification was and still is evidenced in many ways which in the light of what has been said about the total system may be anticipated. Negroes who later came to own slaves were known to treat them more cruelly than some whites. It is manifest in the attempts all too often exaggerated and ludicrous to imitate the White in dress, speech and manners. At present it is most noticeable in crude attempts at hair straightening and the more subtle endeavors of "successful" negroes at progressive whitening over generations by "marrying white."

Force is a very uncertain instrument with which to maintain a society and societies founded wholly and solely on force sooner or later disintegrate. Later West Indian society shifted from control by naked force to a more subtle and permanent integration based upon acceptance by all sections of the superiority of whiteness and white values. The social structure that emerged was a very rigid one with white at the top, black at the bottom, and a confusion of shades in between. But generally the more closely skin color approached white, the nearer the individual was to the top of the status system and vice-versa. This rigid structure was reinforced by the concentration of economic power in the hands of the white minority. This confluence of economic power and a social status system based upon so obvious a characteristic as skin color is a most formidable combination. The acceptance of the superiority of whiteness was to play a most important role in maintaining the rigid social structure, as were the lack of initiative, the immaturity, and irresponsibility that had now become an integral part of the West Indian Negro personality. At this stage of development, the Negro was no longer putting on an act in the interest of survival. These traits, however undesirable we may think them, were part and parcel of his personality. This is not to deny that there were West Indian negroes who displayed initiative, creative energy and leadership. But it was generally accepted that a black person did not aspire to reach the top of the society. On the other hand, a display of too much initiative and leadership was a sign that the individual was issuing a challenge to the established social hierarchy.

In an attempt to illuminate our present position and seek a path by which to know ourselves use has been made of the past. The question is, how far into the past should such an exercise be carried? At this juncture it is opportune to issue an oblique challenge to those who would "return to Africa." It could conceivably be useful to "return to Africa" (note not mother Africa or father Africa) but with a difference of emphasis and intention. The force that molded the West Indian Negro is the plantation. We have had some insights into the way the plantation has shaped the West Indian negro. Most regrettably, it has made him a creature without pride in his color, without dignity and self-respect. The West Indian negro is sorely in need of self-respect, in need to take pride in himself and his achievements. From this point of view exercises in African History might be relevant and important in teaching the West Indian Negro to have pride in the accomplishments of the Black man. But they are not altogether crucial. They throw very little light on our present position. To search Africa for a West Indian identity is a futile exercise. We already have an identity – perhaps none too favorable or self-flattering, but one nonetheless. It is sheer self-hypnotism to believe that if we turn our backs on the West Indies and our eyes to Africa this image would be automatically erased. Once we understand the forces against which the West Indian Negro has had and still has to fight we can be justly proud of our achievements.

    It is very important for those of us, who are in a position to appreciate the forces at work, to emancipate ourselves and then show others the way to freedom. Instead we tend to indulge in patterns of behavior that indicate our subscription to the superiority of whiteness and only serve to reinforce a rigid social structure. Too often the hope of the West Indian Negro is to rise in the social scale and enjoy the social prestige and privileges that have long been associated with a white skin. But always his ambitions are as obvious as his black skin. Inevitably he encounters the barriers that have been erected in order to maintain a rigid social structure and white superiority. Frustrated in his aspirations he indulges in all sorts of rationalizations. Such usually is the nature of Back to Africa utterances. Cries of Colonialism, Imperialism and neo-imperialism, etc. – they are the ritualistic facades behind which a crushing disappointment in and the obsession with the trappings rather than the substance of Independence are hidden, as can be shown by the speed with which former anti-colonists are absorbed into the social circles of former adversaries once it is thought expedient to grant them entry. What we need to do at this crucial stage of our development is to take stock of our present position using the historical past as an objective frame of reference, dispassionately assess and coolly analyze the forces that have shaped us, and on the basis of our findings chart a positive and meaningful course along which our society can be persuaded to move.

**Castine Quashie is a sociologist by training. He works in the corporate sector in St. Vincent and the Grenadines.**

# 30 .SOME FACTS ABOUT YUGOSLAVIA

By Oskar Novak

(Taken from Flambeau, Number 9, July 1968)

Yugoslavia is one of those few relatively small countries which are continually trying to go their own way towards a better, truly humanistic socialist society. In a world where the cold war is still going on, it seems to be a rather difficult way.

Partly because of their strong determination to go towards socialism and partly because the Yugoslavs believe that there are different ways in doing so, heavy criticism is thrown upon them both from the right and the extreme left of the international political scene. As a result of this the newspaper reader will find many different and controversial opinions about the Yugoslavs experience in the gossip columns of the international press. Recognizing that hardly any of those opinions are ever based on facts he eventually gets bored with the whole issue. But he is no fool – he sometimes makes an effort to get the facts before arriving at an opinion. This short article is aimed at presenting facts and allowing the reader to make his own interpretation.

## GEOGRAPHIC POSITIONS AND HISTORICAL BACKGROUND

The country is located in the south part of Central Europe surrounded by Italy, Austria, Hungary, Romania, Bulgaria, Greece, Albania and the Adriatic Sea. About twenty million inhabitants live in the country's 255,807 square kilometers. Under the name Yugoslavia the state was established by a union between Serbia, Croatia and Slovenia in 1918 into a Kingdom which went, in the eyes of the people, into economic, moral and political bankruptcy before the Second World War. After the peoples of the country had really been united in the war against their common enemy – Hitler's Germany – immediately after the war, in the first general elections, they decided to declare the republic. Under the leadership of the undoubtedly greatest personality in their history, of the organizer of the resistance movement and of the liberation army and the leaders of the Communist Party – Josip Broz Tito – the state developed to its present day form of Socialist Federative Republic of Yugoslavia.

## SOCIAL AND POLITICAL ORGANIZATION

The fast post war changes in the social structure have been followed by changes in the Constitution in 1953 and 1963. According to the Constitution of 1963, the state is a federation of six republics and two autonomous provinces which have equal rights and far reaching independence in matters of economic and cultural life. The republics again consist of a great number of communes which are usually the towns or other centers of economic activity together with the surrounding areas. The communes have the constitutional right of self-government through local authorities and they are responsible for economic development, education and cultural activities, health and social services in their territory.

The Communal Assembly is the basic unit of parliamentary democracy in Yugoslavia. Every member of the society, regardless of formal membership of any political organization, is eligible to be nominated for a seat in the Communal, Republican or Federal Assembly. The nomination of candidates takes place during the meetings of the voters of the territorial units. Any ten citizens can propose a candidate. The members of the Communal Assembly are elected in local elections. The Communal Assembly then approves the candidates nominated by the voters for seats in the Republican and Federal Assemblies and these MP's are elected in republican and general elections. Any post in an Assembly (local, republican or federal) can be held only for four years. Elections are so timed that every two years, half of the MP's in the Assemblies (on all levels) are changed.

The Republican Assemblies and the Federal Assembly have four chambers according to the main fields of social activity (business, education and culture, health and social care, and local self-government). It has been found that such a specialization of the MP's is necessary for effective and competent legislation which is entirely in the hands of the Assemblies. The Federal and Republican Assemblies have their Executive Councils which are regarded as the Federal and Republican Governments. These Governments are responsible for their policies to the nts are responsible for their policies to the Assemblies. The President of the Federal Executive Council must be approved by the President of the Republic.

The concept of self-government is consequently applied in all fields of social activity. All firms and institutions in the economy and in any other kind of employment are managed through the system of workers' self-management. The "workers councils" have the right and responsibility to run the enterprises and institutions in business and elsewhere.

Once one realizes that socialism is the generally accepted target of the development of the Yugoslav society, that there are no controversial class interests, and that active part in ruling the country is secured by his constitutional right of self government (on his job and where he lives), it is obvious that there is no ground and justification for the existence of the classical political parties. Indeed, the previous Communist Party does not act any more as such. Today the League of Communists forms an avantgarde of the population which have the willingness and ability to give creative support and special contributions for the achievement of the objectives of their society as a whole. The League of Communists and the various youth, veteran and women organizations are all constituents of the Socialist Alliance of the Working People which has a long tradition inherited from the war time National Front.

## THE ECONOMIC SYSTEM

Immediately after the war, all the means of production were nationalized, except in agriculture where a suitable amount of land was given to every peasant family. The entire economy was state owned and managed through operational planning by government agencies and ministries. In fact, that kind of state socialism was not very different from the usual forms of state ownership of enterprises both in the East and West, and as such falls short of Yugoslavia's ideals. That is why in 1950 the state ownership of the firms was abandoned. The means of production (the existing firms and the society's capital and natural resources) remained public property but the right to operate and manage them on behalf of the community has been given to the workers employed in the firms. The worker's councils elected from the workers in the firm virtually run the firms. These workers councils have their operative Managing Boards. All departments of the firm are responsible to the council. To reach the optimal long- and short-term business decisions, the workers councils use the service of the various specialized departments of the firm (market research and forecasting, investment project evaluation, etc.)

For quite a long time, this system of workers management in the economy has not been consistent enough with the practice of economic planning in the country. Although the workers councils had all the necessary formal rights through the high level of taxation a redistribution of income in favor of the state has been maintained because centralized economic planning could not have been carried out without centralized disposal of the investment funds. In that way the effectiveness of the workers management has been limited by the amount of net revenue left to the firms after taxation.

As soon as the fundamental steps in the industrialization of the country had been completed, it became obvious that for the further steady growth of the economy, the use of the market forces and of the market mechanism in combination with the decision-making freedom of the workers councils can be more effective than the essentially administrative central planning of all details of economic activity. So, gradually, the supply and demand forces in the market have been allowed to determine the prices in most sectors and economic panning concentrated itself on the main targets of the country's development policy. The emphasis has been given to the quality of planning a framework for economic growth, inside which the freedom of the enterprises can be maintained. Instead of administrative regulations the achievement of the objectives of the economy policy is now secured by economic measures (monetary and fiscal policy, exchange rate control, tariffs, etc.)

Economic planning is being conducted on three main levels, in the enterprises in local and republican Assemblies and in the Federal Assembly. The workers councils are responsible for the preparation of the plans of the enterprises. Local authorities combine the plans of the enterprises in their territory, eliminating duplications and overlapping of the individual plans, and fulfilling the gaps where necessary with their funds. Between the local, republican and federal authorities there is a two way cooperation and exchange of information in the process of planning. The plan of the Federation sets the main targets of development. There are short term (for 1-2 years), intermediate term (for 5-7 years), and long term (for 15-20 years) development plans.

To introduce this system of economic planning and market mechanism, in 1961 and 1965 a whole range of measures of economic policy has been employed. These are usually referred to as "economic reform" Those measures aim to redistribute the national income between the enterprises and the state in such a way as to secure the necessary means for the independent business policies of the firms run by their workers councils.

## SOME OF THE RESULTS OF THE POST-WAR DEVELOPMENT

Before one can judge the achievements of the post-war Yugoslavia, it must be recognized that during the war the major part of the economy was destroyed. It took four years of fighting before the Yugoslavs got rid of Hitler's armies, and 1.7 million of their citizens (or 10 percent of the entire population at that time) had been killed. Another thing to remember is that after 1948 (almost until 1955) a severe economic blockage was imposed upon them by East Europe. It is estimated that that blockage slowed down the rate of economic growth for as much as 30 percent at that time.

In spite of all this, an average annual rate of growth of real national income of 7 percent for the time period 1948-1963 has been achieved. The rate of growth has been much faster after 1953 (9 percent a year between 1953 and 1963). After 1957 the growth of the Yugoslav economy (10 percent a year between 1957 and 1963) has been second only to Japan in the world.

It is even more important that at the same time the structure of the economy has been transformed from a mainly agricultural society in the prewar period (with over 75 percent of the population living on the agriculture) to a moderately industrialized country (with less than 78 percent of agricultural population). While industry produced only 29.7 percent of the country's gross national produce in 1949, its share increased to 48.3 percent in 1964.

The per capita national income reached 500 dollars a year in 1963. Because of the public ownership of the means of production the distribution of income follows the principle that everybody should earn only according to his personal contribution to the society – according to the efficiency of his own work. This allows a much more even distribution of income and a better standard of living for the great majority of the people than in many rich countries.

The specific economic system and planning mechanism allowed for special care concerning the most underdeveloped areas of the country. Great efforts to create new employment and faster economic growth in such regions, through income redistribution from the richer to the poorer areas and through encouragement of investment in the latter, considerable success has been achieved.

The entire education is free with eight years of compulsory education on the primary level. Before the war, Yugoslavia had 26 institutions of high education (university facilities, high schools and colleges, technical institutes and arts academies) with 16,798 students in the academic year 1938-39. In 1965-66 the number of those institutions was 226 with 184,923 students.

Similarly, all institutions of the "welfare state" are operating in Yugoslavia for a long time. Family allowances, old age pensions, unemployment payments, free health service, etc., are all provided. The Yugoslavs just do not boast about it so much because they feel all this is quite natural to have in a socialist country.

## RELATIONS WITH OTHER COUNTRIES

As a result of its tradition, geographical position and fast post - war economic growth, Yugoslavia is widely engaged in international economic relations. Trade relations are being maintained with more than a hundred countries, regardless of their political orientation. As in foreign policy, so in international economic relations, Yugoslavia is non-aligned. So far it has been found that it is impossible for her to join any of the existing regional economic integrations because their policy implications are inconsistent with the Yugoslav non -aligned position.

Yugoslavia is a very active member of such international economic organizations as General Agreement on Tariffs and Trade, United Nations Conference on Trade and Development, United Nations Economic Commission for Europe and Organization for Economic Cooperation and Development, helping the efforts of young developing countries for the creation of free trade in the world as a whole and for the abolition of discriminating against developing and non-aligned countries in the world markets.

In the purely political field, Yugoslavia is even more non-aligned. She is not a member of any military or defense organization or pact. Her relations with other countries are maintained under the recognition of her principles of national independence and political sovereignty, territorial integrity and peaceful international coexistence and cooperation through the United Nations. Many principles formulated in the First Conference of Non-Aligned Countries held in Yugoslavia (Belgrade) in 1961 are nowadays universally accepted.